THE

LIGHT OF PROPHECY

LET IN ON THE DARK PLACES OF

THE PAPACY:

BEING

AN EXPOSITION OF 2D THESSAL. II. 3—12.

SHOWING ITS EXACT FULFILMENT IN THE CHURCH OF ROME,
WITH SPECIAL REFERENCE TO
THE ASPECT OF THAT CHURCH IN THE PRESENT DAY.

BY THE

REV. ALEXANDER HISLOP,
MINISTER OF THE EAST FREE CHURCH, ARBROATH.

EDINBURGH:
WILLIAM WHYTE AND CO.,
BOOKSELLERS TO THE QUEEN DOWAGER.
ARBROATH: P. WILSON; S. GELLATLY; AND J. ADAM.
LONDON: LONGMAN AND CO. DUBLIN:
W. CURRY, JUN. AND CO.

MDCCCXLVI.

TO

DAVID DAVIDSON, Esq.,

OF STRATH,

This little Work,

DESIGNED TO

AID IN EXPOSING A SYSTEM,

OF WHICH HE HAS LONG BEEN THE FIRM AND

ENLIGHTENED OPPONENT,

IS,

WITH EVERY SENTIMENT OF RESPECT AND REGARD,

INSCRIBED BY HIS AFFECTIONATE FRIEND,

THE AUTHOR.

PREFACE.

The one grand question of the day is now manifestly Popery. The Prime Minister of Great Britain has declared his intention to endow the Romish priesthood of Ireland as soon as he finds it convenient; and it is but too plain that the heads of the different political parties are quite ready to give him their support in carrying his design into effect. The friends of Protestant truth may therefore be looking forward to a conflict on this subject at no distant day.

To prepare the country for the coming struggle, it is essential that the public mind be thoroughly enlightened as to the nature of the system which it is now proposed to endow. Much has been already written on the subject of Popery, and ably and well. But a succinct and yet comprehensive view of the leading features of Romanism, as delineated by the unerring pencil of inspiration, and reflected not only in the history of the past, but above all in the events of the *present day*, is, at this moment, a desideratum. The following pages are intended as a contribution, in some measure, to supply the desideratum.

Most of the work now presented to the reader was written before the recent elevation of Pius IX. to the chair of St Peter. But notwithstanding the praises that have been heaped on the new Pontiff from all quarters, as if he were destined to cleanse the Augean stable, the author has seen nothing in all the much-lauded sayings or doings of his Holiness that required him to change or to modify a single statement as to the Antichristian principles or practices of Rome. Pius has indeed departed, in some respects, from the beaten track of his predecessors; but the changes which he has either made or announced, are changes merely of administration, not of principle—changes that may make some little difference in the secular management of the Roman States, but do not at all affect either the doctrine or discipline of the Romish Church. His Holiness has relaxed on the subject of railroads; but he has relaxed nothing on the far more vital subject of liberty of conscience. One of the latest acts of his that have transpired, is his "condemning and proscribing into the Index Expurgatorius," four new works, two of which are translations of the Gospels, one into French, the other into Italian. Those, therefore, who expect any real reformation from Rome, are looking for grapes from thorns, and figs from thistles. Popery may change its phase, but never changes its nature. It is always the Mystery of iniquity; and not less so, because his Holiness has the art to dazzle the eyes of the world by seeming concessions, and splendid acts of clemency, which are both fitted and intended to bind his subjects the more firmly in the bonds of spiritual despotism.

Individual cardinals may feel, or affect to feel,

antipathy to some of his measures; but there can be no doubt that his policy has the full sympathy of the "Sacred College," in which, it is well known, the rankest principles of Jesuitism have long been predominant. The very fact that one so young (his Holiness being only 54) has been UNANIMOUSLY elected by the Holy Fathers, and that in the brief space of two days, while it demonstrates the entire agreement of his views in all essential points with their own, is at the same time a strong indication that in *their* estimation he must be possessed of more than ordinary abilities for gaining for these views the approbation and acceptance of the world.

Oct. 5, 1846.

CONTENTS.

CHAPTER I.

The Apostacy.

2 THESSALONIANS ii. 3.

"Let no man deceive you by any means: for that day shall not come, except there come a falling away first."

IF there were no other prophecy in the New Testament than that which is contained in this Epistle, it would be sufficient of itself to prove the Divine origin of Christianity. The description which it gives of the principles and practices of the Church of Rome, as developed in its whole history, is so clear, so graphic, and minute, that it is impossible to account for the coincidence on any other supposition than that the writer was inspired. A comparison of the prediction with its fulfilment is eminently fitted, under the Divine blessing, to confirm the faith of the Christian, to confound the scepticism of the infidel, and even to open the eyes of Romanists themselves.

The occasion which called forth the prophecy may be found on the face of the Epistle. A persuasion, arising either from a misunderstanding of certain expressions of Paul's in his former Epistle, or from the circulation of forged Epistles in Paul's name, had laid hold of the minds of many among the Thessalonians, that the day of the Lord was at hand, and that the world was about to come to an end. The effect of this was, that some were unduly alarmed, while others, under pretence, perhaps, of superior regard for the things of eternity, neglected their worldly business, and gave themselves up to idleness. To remedy both evils, the Apostle informs them that many events were to take place, and great and disastrous changes to happen to the visible church, before the great day of the Lord should come. "Let no man deceive you by any means," said he; "for that day shall not come, except there come a falling away first," or more literally, "except THE APOSTACY* come first."

The falling away, the apostacy, of which the Apostle here speaks, was to be no slight, no isolated departure from the faith. It was to be a wide-spread and general defection. Our Lord himself had foretold such an apostacy, when iniquity should abound, when the love of the many should wax cold, when false Christs and false prophets should arise, and error should appear in such subtle and plausible shapes "as to deceive, if it were possible, the very elect." The partizans of the Papacy, indeed, in their pride, claim for their church an entire exemption from any such danger. Whatever church may err, whatever church may fall away, the Church of Rome, say they, cannot. Because Christ said to *Peter*, "I have prayed for *thee*, that thy faith fail not,"—and again, "Thou art Peter; and on this rock will I build my church, and the gates

* ἡ ἀποστασία.

of hell shall not prevail against it,"*—they leap to the conclusion that *Rome* is infallible, that *Rome* is incapable of apostacy. Thus they fondly delude themselves. But certain it is that Paul attached no such meaning to the language of Christ as they do. *He* regarded not the Roman church as beyond the danger of fatal defection. Listen to his own words, as addressed to that very church :—" Boast not against the branches. But if thou boast, thou bearest not the root, but the root thee. Thou wilt say then, The branches were broken off that I might be graffed in. Well: because of unbelief they were broken off, and thou standest by faith. Be not high-minded, but fear. For if God spared not the natural branches, take heed lest he also spare not thee. Behold therefore the goodness and severity of God: on them which fell, severity: but towards thee goodness, if thou continue in his goodness: *otherwise thou also shalt be cut off.*"† The Spirit by which Paul was inspired saw the lurking

* See Note A. † Rom. xi. 18—22.

pride and high-mindedness of the Roman church, while yet in its infancy, and gave it solemn warning of its danger. But the warning was in vain. It *did* fall away, and that speedily. Chrysostom, at the end of the fourth century, comparing its former state with what it then was, lamented its declension from the position which it occupied when "the apostles of Christ suffered martyrdom in it, and left their whole doctrine to it." "It was a happy church then," said he; "but now, O Rome, how much art thou changed from the old Rome! Thou which hast been the chief in all the world art now the chief in all wickedness."

Such is the testimony of Chrysostom as to the early declension of the Church of Rome; but the Apostle will himself best explain what he means by "the apostacy." In the First Epistle to Timothy he has given us some of its leading characteristics; and these at once identify it as a *Roman* apostacy. "The Spirit speaketh expressly, that in the latter times some shall depart (in the original, *apostatize**) from the faith, giving heed to seducing spirits, and doctrines of devils (more literally 'doctrines concerning *demons*†), speaking lies in hypocrisy, having their consciences seared with a hot iron, forbidding to marry, and commanding to abstain from meats, which God hath created to be received with thanksgiving."‡ Here we have four distinct and unequivocal marks of the Papal church.

1. "The doctrines concerning demons." It has been shown in the most satisfactory manner by Mede, Tillotson, and Newton, that the doctrines here referred to are none other than those tenets of the Romish system which inculcate the worship of departed saints, and which occupy so conspicuous a place in the creed of that church. Popery has been called "baptised Paganism;"

* ἀποστήσονται.

† διδασκαλίαις δαιμονίων. If any one think this an unnatural construction, let him consult Heb. vi. 2, where he will find βαπτισμῶν διδαχῆ used in the same sense.

‡ 1 Tim. iv. 1—3.

and the way in which the demons of the heathen have been adopted by Rome, under Christian names, amply justifies the title. The saints of the Romish calendar have in all respects succeeded to the place and divine honours of the demons of heathenism. To an English ear, indeed, the name *demon* always conveys an unfavourable idea. It was not so among the ancients. Now, what were the demons of Pagan antiquity? Plato will tell us:—"When good men die," says that philosopher,—and he only echoes the sentiment of Hesiod before him,*—"when good men die, they attain to great honour and dignity, and become *demons*," i. e. deified men.† Thus Hercules and Bacchus, and Castor and Pollux, and a crowd of other departed heroes, were, for their real, or fancied merits, enrolled among the minor deities of Greece and Rome. Nay, women were deified as well as men. To these male and female divinities altars were reared, temples consecrat-

* Hesiod's Works and Days, lib. i. 120.
† Plat. Cratylus, p. 398, tom. i.

ed, sacrifice and incense offered, and all manner of divine honours duly paid. And just so is it with the departed saints in the Church of Rome. The *canonization* of the saints is neither more nor less than the *apotheosis* of the illustrious departed of heathenism. St Peter and St Thomas, and St Augustine, and Mary, with her train of virgins, have only usurped the honours of the deified men and women of classical antiquity. Nay, as if the more clearly to identify Popery with this mark of the apostacy, the Church of Rome has actually so far forgotten herself, as to bestow the very name which signifies a demon, or deified person, upon her saints. *Divus* in Latin, is identical with *demon* in Greek; and this of all others is the name which Rome has bestowed upon her most illustrious saints. Of this any one may satisfy himself, who looks into the works of the Latin fathers published by the Church of Rome, and compares the titles bestowed upon these fathers, with those bestowed by the Pagans upon their deified emperors. hus, the ancient Romans spoke of their departed emperors, as *Divus Julius, Divus Augustus, &c.* the deified Julius, the deified Augustus, &c.; and in precisely the same manner do the Papists speak of their saints as *Divus Cyprianus, Divus Augustinus,* the deified Cyprian, the deified Augustine.

Now, while the saints of the Romish Church thus bear the same name, and receive the same divine honours as the heathen demons, they are believed by their infatuated worshippers to perform the same offices as their ancient prototypes did. "Every demon," says Plato, "is a middle being between God and mortal man. All the commerce and intercourse between God and man is carried on by the *mediation* of demons. Demons are reporters and carriers from men to the gods, and again from the gods to men, of the supplications and sacrifices of the one, and of the injunctions and rewards of sacrifices, from the other."* Such was the office of the Pagan demons; the office of the saints in the Romish

* Plat. Sympo. pp. 202, 203, tom. iii. apud Newton.

calendar is exactly the same. They are *mediators* between heaven and earth. To them especially prayers are addressed, and through their intercession, all benefits are obtained. Although the word of God expressly declares, that as there is only "one God," so is there only "one Mediator between God and man," Papists have added other mediators without number, who have usurped the place of God's only begotten Son. Thus is Pagan idolatry unblushingly engrafted by Rome upon the Christian Church. The Papists, indeed, try to shift from themselves the odium of the charge of idolatry, by subtle distinctions, about supreme and relative worship, about the *kind* of worship due to God, and that due to their canonized mediators. But in order to prove that their church has in this respect utterly apostatized from the faith of the gospel, we have no need to puzzle ourselves with their superfine and quibbling distinctions; we have not the least occasion to inquire whether the worship they bestow upon the saints, is Dulia or Latria. Whatever it be, it is manifest, that they give the same honour to these saints, as the heathen did to their demons. This is a fact, which is *substantially* admitted by themselves, and by those who are recognized as authorities among them. Thus, for instance, speaks Theodoret, one of the fathers, who had a great hand in bringing this idolatry into the church:—"The martyrs have blotted out of the minds of men," says he, addressing the Pagans, "the memory of those who were called gods. For our Lord hath brought *his dead into the place of your gods*, whom he hath utterly abolished, and hath *given their honours to the martyrs;* for instead of the festivals of Jupiter and Bacchus, are now celebrated the festivals of Peter, and Paul, and Thomas, and the other martyrs."* The inscriptions on many of the Roman Catholic churches testify the very same thing. For instance, at Rome, on the spot where there anciently stood a temple to Mars, there is now erected a church to St Martina, with an inscription, which is thus render-

* Theodoret. Serm. 8. De Martyribus, pp. 606, 607.

ed in English, by Dr Conyers Middleton, in his famous "Letter from Rome."

> "Mars hence expelled, Martina martyred maid
> Claims the same worship, as to him was paid."

"Whatever worship," adds Dr Middleton, "was paid by the ancients to their heroes, or inferior deities, the Romans now pay to their saints and martyrs, as their own inscriptions do plainly declare; which, like those of St Martina and the Pantheon, generally signify, that the honours, which of old had been impiously given in that place to the false god, are now piously and rightly transferred to the Christian saint; or, as one of their celebrated poets expresses himself, in regard to St George:—

> 'As Mars our fathers once adored, so now
> To thee, O George, we humbly prostrate bow.'"*

Thus, then, with regard to saint-worship in general, the Church of Rome has, beyond all question, this brand of the apostacy predicted by Paul, that it worships human mediators, just as the heathen worshipped their *demons*. But

* Letter from Rome, p. 177.

there is *one* of these mediators that stands pre-eminent above all the rest, and receives a blasphemous homage, about the character of which there cannot possibly be a doubt; and that is the Virgin Mary. In the breviary, she is styled the "Queen of Heaven," and "mistress of all the creatures;" churches are dedicated to her, with inscriptions, which put her on a level with the Godhead; and language is addressed to her, which cannot, without the grossest impiety, be addressed to any created being. "At Ariceia," says a recent traveller, "the worship of Diana is now superseded by that of the Virgin. Over the door of the church, dedicated to her, is this inscription in Latin, so shocking to the eye of a Protestant, *Sacred to Mary, equal to God the Father!* This inscription is also seen on one of the churches in the Corso at Rome, and in many others in Italy."* That this is no unmeaning language is plain, from the way in which she is celebrated in the most favourite works of devo-

* Three Years in Italy, 1828.

tion in the Romish Church:—"Come unto Mary," says St Bonaventure, blasphemously parodying the most touching passages in the Bible; "Come unto Mary, all ye that labour and are heavy laden, and she shall refresh your souls. Come unto her in your temptations, and the serenity of her countenance shall establish you. O lady, in thee do I put my trust, deliver my soul from mine enemies. O give thanks unto the Lord, for he is good. O give thanks unto his Mother, for her mercy endureth for ever."* And as if it were not blasphemy enough to put a creature in the same rank as the Creator, they even take a higher flight, and exalt the Virgin *above* Christ himself. "More present relief," says St Anselm, "is sometimes found by commemorating the name of Mary, than by calling upon the name of our Lord Jesus Christ."† "Often," says St Bernardine, "those whom the justice of the Son might condemn, the mercy of the mother delivers;" and therefore he ex-

* M'Culloch, Pop. Cond., pp. 337, 338.
† Usher's Answer to a Jesuit, p. 495.

horts the sinner to "appeal from the court of God's justice to the court of his mother's mercy."* "Oh! empress, and our most kind lady," says St Bonaventure, "by the authority of a mother, *command* thy beloved Son our Lord Jesus Christ, that he would vouchsafe to lift up our minds from the love of earthly things unto heavenly desires."† Such are extracts from the most favourite devotional writers in the Church of Rome, and the language of the pontiff who died only the other day, is not a whit less blasphemous. In his Encyclical Letter, published on the 15th August 1832, addressed to "all patriarchs, primates, archbishops, and bishops," after denouncing "liberty of conscience" as a "most pestilential error," and "that worst and never sufficiently to be execrated and detested liberty of the press," and calling upon all to whom he wrote "faithfully to discharge their duty" for the suppression of heresy, Pope Gregory thus concludes:

* Bernardinus in Mariali apud Jewell on Thessalonians, p. 209.

† Usher's Answer, p. 486.

"But that all may have a successful issue, let us raise our eyes to the most blessed Virgin, who ALONE destroys heresies, who is our GREATEST hope; yea, the ENTIRE GROUND of our hope!"* Thus Christ Jesus is entirely stripped of his inalienable dignity as Mediator; that one who, though washed and sanctified, was yet conceived in sin and shapen in iniquity, might be placed on the mediatorial throne in his stead. It was the condemnation of the heathen that "they worshipped and served the creature more than the Creator, who is over all blessed for ever." The church that countenances the ascription of such honours as the above to any mere human being, is implicated in the very same guilt. It is impossible, then, to resist the conclusion that in the Church of Rome is to be found that apostacy which was to be characterized by giving heed to seducing spirits and "doctrines concerning demons," or the deified spirits of the departed. The next mark is equally characteristic,

2. "Speaking lies in hypocrisy." Popery is

* Protestant Magazine, No. 50, p. 43, 1843.

one system of lying and imposture from beginning to end. It sprung from the father of lies, and in every period of its history it has had recourse to his favourite artifices. The relics, which are exhibited in its churches, testify that it is bolstered up by fraud and falsehood. Many different churches in different parts of the world are in possession of the very same relics. In Flanders, Spain, and France, there are eight arms of Matthew the Evangelist; besides the holy coat at Trèves, there are twenty-two other holy coats, all equally genuine, all equally holy; and as for the wood of the true cross, it is so abundant, that, as has been said, it would suffice to build a frigate of 74 guns, or supply a town with fuel for a winter. Nor is it only in the darker parts of Europe that such impostures are practised. The Archbishop of Paris has recently *discovered* a fund of most precious relics, which he has publicly called on the people of his diocese to *come and adore*. In the bill, announcing the discovery to the inhabitants of the French capital, a copy of which I have myself seen, the following are among the articles enumerated: A bit of our Saviour's crown of thorns, some of the nails with which he was fastened to the cross, the iron lance that pierced his side, the spunge that contained the vinegar given him to drink, the reed put into his hand for a sceptre, a piece of the real sepulchre, and the towel with which he wiped the apostles' feet!! * These and many more are exhibited by this high authority to the Papists of France, as veritable and genuine relics. What man of common sense does not see that this necessarily implies lying and imposture of the rankest kind? But "pious frauds" have ever been regarded as a legitimate means of advancing the interests and building up the power of the Romish Church. Papists in the present day are found to deny the charge,

* When the fact above mentioned was stated by that excellent man, the Rev. F. Monod, in Edinburgh last year, Bishop Gillies attacked M. Monod, and attempted to explain away the adoration; but for a whole year he never ventured to look at the Reply from that gentleman, which his letter called forth. He has at last issued a pamphlet on the subject; but it leaves the matter exactly as he found it.

but in vain. The truth of it is indelibly stamped on the page of authentic history. In Scotland such unholy means of propagating Popery were clearly brought to light in the reign of James VI.* The immediate occasion of the swearing of the National Covenant was the interception of letters from Rome, granting a dispensation to the Scottish Roman Catholics to make a profession of Protestantism for a time, provided they preserved an inward attachment to the faith, and embraced every opportunity of advancing it in secret. In England a precisely similar discovery had been made a few years before. In 1568, one Thomas Heth, who passed himself off for a poor Protestant minister, had been allowed to preach on trial in the Cathedral of Rochester. At the end of the service, a letter which had dropped from his pocket while preaching, was found in the bottom of the pulpit by the sexton, and carried to the dean. This letter, which was addressed to Heth, under a fictitious name, by a noted Jesuit at Madrid, re-

* M'Crie's Life of Melville, vol. i. p. 262.

vealed him at once, in his true character, as a Popish priest. Immediately a search being made in his lodgings, in one of his boots were found his beads, a license from the society of the Jesuits, and a bull of Pope Pius V., giving him authority to preach whatever doctrine might be deemed most suitable for sowing disunion among the English Protestants.*

Now, does any one suppose that the Church of Rome has abandoned all such procedure in modern times? The course pursued by Mr Newman gives every reason to conclude the reverse. There are the strongest grounds for believing, that that ringleader of the Tractarians was from the first a *bona fide* Jesuit in concert with the Vatican. It is well known that when the Tracts were first commenced, while they displayed a most unequivocal Romeward *tendency*, they at the same time contained many things condemnatory of Rome. Was this because the writers were convinced that Rome was deserving of the censure bestowed on her? No, in nowise.

* The Protestant, vol. iii. p. 287.

Why then did they speak with such severity of a church which they latterly took every opportunity of lauding to the skies? Let Mr Newman himself answer. "SUCH VIEWS WERE NECESSARY FOR OUR POSITION."* It was necessary, at the outset, by all means, to blind the public as to the ultimate tendency of Tractarian principles. At the time when Mr Newman made this avowal that precaution was necessary no longer. Protestant prejudices had been broken down. The horror of Popery was worn off; and it was needless any longer to wear a mask. But from his own statement it is plain that he must have been a Papist at first, as much as when he actually seceded to Rome. Whatever may have been the reason that led him at last to leave the Church of England, *conscience* it could not be. A man who could lay down the doctrine as to lying, which he has done, can have little pretension to a conscience. "The Christian," says Mr Newman, quoting Clement of Alexandria with high approbation, "the Christian both

* Dublin Christian Examiner, No. 7, January 1844.

thinks and speaks the truth, *except when consideration is necessary;* and then, as a physician for the good of his patients, he will be false, or utter a falsehood, as the sophists say. Nothing, however, but his neighbour's good will lead him to do this. *He gives himself up for the church.*"* That is, in other words, there are no falsehoods which he may not legitimately tell whenever the good of the church may seem to require it. Mr Newman is now an *avowed* Papist; and his conduct is one more proof that the Church of Rome is that apostate church, which, according to Paul, was to be distinguished by its members speaking lies in hypocrisy, having their consciences seared with a hot iron.

But is Mr Newman singular in this respect in the present day? How, then, are we to account for the gross inconsistency between the practice and profession of O'Connell, the champion of Irish Catholicity? When the tide ran strong against all religious endowments, he pro-

* Newman's "Arians of the Fourth Century," p. 72, apud Christian's Monthly Magazine, No. II.

fessed most loudly to coincide with the popular feeling. What, for instance, could be stronger than the following in his letter to Mr Buchan of Kelloe:—"I say it with all the solemnity, though without the formality of an oath—I say it in the presence of that God before whom you and I shall shortly stand, you would not be more disposed to resist the exaltation of my church to temporal wealth and power, than I should be, and am." And yet a few weeks had not passed away before that same man was found in his place in Parliament, battling for an endowment, and an *exclusive* endowment to the Popish priests in the proposed workhouses in Ireland; and ever since, he has been straining every nerve to get one endowment after another bestowed on that corrupt church of which he is a member. If this was not speaking lies in hypocrisy, what is? What else also was the conduct of Dr Murray, the Roman Catholic Archbishop of Dublin, when he, a few years ago, to serve a purpose, made such professions of liberality towards his Protestant countrymen? At the very time that he was *publicly* addressing the Protestants as "beloved fellow-Christians," he was *privately* engaged in promoting the circulation, among his clergy, of the atrocious work of Peter Dens, in which all Protestants are consigned, as heretics, to merciless destruction here, and everlasting perdition hereafter. That work, which was *dedicated* to him by Coyne, the publisher, in 1832, as having been "UNDERTAKEN WITH HIS APPROBATION,"* which was recommended by him, along with the other prelates of the Irish Roman Catholic church, as a text-book for the clergy, lays it down in express terms, that liberty of conscience or religion "is certainly false and condemned,—that it is not to be tried or approved, but to be *extirpated, unless there may be some prudential reasons which may induce us to tolerate it,*"†—that all baptized persons, to

* "Ejus cum approbatione susceptam." See this whole subject ably discussed in Church of Scotland Magazine, vol. ii., p. 316.

† Dens' Theology, vol. ii. p. 83.

whatever denomination they may belong, "can be compelled, by corporeal punishment, to return to the Catholic faith,"*—and that if all other means fail, "*they should be put to death.*"† Yet these same heretics did Dr Murray address as "beloved fellow-Christians"!

There is no other church in the world in w ich lying is so systematically practised as in the Church of Rome. And no wonder that the practice is so common, when we learn the authorised doctrine of that church with regard to oaths. "A vow or oath," says Dens, "is taken away or relaxed by the superiors of the Church, IN THE PLACE OF GOD, and so the obligation thence arising spontaneously ceases, by the removal of the matter"!‡ When men claim this power to dispense with the solemn obligation of an oath, and to give warrant whenever they please for the commission of perjury, the respect for truth must be at the lowest possible ebb. Pope Clement VI., in 1347, granted to

* Dens' Theology, vol. ii. p. 80. † Ibid. p. 89.
‡ Ibid. p. 272.

John and Joan, king and queen of France, and their successors for ever, a perpetual indulgence to "break such oaths by them taken, or by them *to be* taken, as they could not profitably keep."* The terms of this dispensation show the wickedness of the system in all its grossness; but the power which, according to Dens, is at this day possessed by every bishop, of "taking away or relaxing oaths," whenever "any reasonable cause," such as "the utility of the Church," demands it, is in reality not less atrocious. What corruption, what wickedness must be the consequence of such a system! But how clearly from all this is it to be seen, that in the Church of Rome are to be found the predicted promoters of the apostacy "who speak lies in hypocrisy, having their consciences seared with a hot iron"! The third mark of the Apostacy is,

3. "Forbidding to marry;" and where is that to be found, if not in the Church of Rome? Although God in paradise before the fall said, "It is not good that man should be alone,"—

* Dacheri. Spicileg. tom. iv. p. 275.

although Christ honoured the marriage of Cana in Galilee with his presence,—although the Holy Ghost declares that "marriage is honourable in all, and the bed undefiled," the Papal church looks down upon matrimony as a state unfit for the holiness of her priesthood, and prohibits all her clergy from ever contracting it. How rigorously this prohibition is enforced, we may learn from an unsuspicious witness, the late Bishop Hay of Edinburgh. In his "Sincere Christian Instructed," we find the following question and answer:—"*Q.* Does the Church oblige all those in sacred orders to live *single* and chaste? *Ans.* This she requires from them in the *strictest manner*, so as to decree the severest penalties against those among them who violate this law; having sometimes ordered them to be deposed, sometimes excommunicated, sometimes to be imprisoned in monasteries, to spend their whole lives in penance." The Papists try to evade this mark of the apostacy, as applying to their Church, by telling us that the Spirit of God, in this passage, had reference to certain ancient heretics, who sprang up very early in the Christian church. But how can this possibly help the Church of Rome, when she is found actually to have adopted the *practice* of these heretics? She "*forbids* to marry," as well as these heretics did, and much more stringently too. And the ground on which celibacy is enforced is most dishonouring to God; for what is the principle on which it is so strictly enjoined on the clergy? The same Bishop Hay will answer. "Because," says he, "a life of purity and chastity is more excellent, more perfect, and more acceptable to God, than the married state." Here it is necessarily implied, that the "married state" is *not* a life of "purity and chastity;" thereby directly reflecting on God who instituted it, on Christ who countenanced it, on the Holy Spirit, who hath pronounced it "honourable in all men." What is this, but either to declare, with the ancient heretics, that "marriage is an invention of the devil," or that the God of holiness has sanctioned an *im*pure and *un*chaste institution? This same principle runs through all the writings of the Roman Catholics on the subject. Nay, not a few of them plainly and positively lay down the principle, that concubinage in a priest is much more innocent than marriage. Cardinal Campeggio, Coster, Albertus Pighius, and many others of their most distinguished writers, have taught, that "the priest who keeps a harlot lives much more chastely and holily than he who has a lawful wife."* The very same doctrine is even introduced into their notes on their Bibles. In the Rhemish Testament, for instance, the following note is to be found:—"We say also concerning others lawfully made priests, and such as otherwise have made vow of chastity: They cannot marry at all, and therefore there is no comparison in them, betwixt marriage and fornication, or burning. For their marriage is but pretended, and is the *worst sort* of incontinency or burning."† And we shall see, in a subsequent part of this treatise, that

* Jewell's Apolog., Part 4th.

† Rhemish Testament. Note on 1 Cor. vii. 9, ed. 1582.

the *practice* of the Church of Rome has been in exact accordance with this doctrine, and that her priests, while abhorring marriage, have been distinguished for licentiousness. Bishop Hay knew this perfectly well; and yet with the hardihood so characteristic of his church, he could pen the following:—"Seeing, therefore, that the office of the priesthood requires the most angelic purity, and the most sublime sanctity, in those who are admitted to it, therefore, the church has judged proper to oblige all who enter into that office, to embrace the more perfect state of chastity." Truly it is plain, that those who "forbid to marry speak lies in hypocrisy."

It is certain that our Lord required no such "sublime sanctity," no such "angelic purity," in the first ministers of Christianity. Peter was a married man; Philip, the evangelist, had four daughters; and Paul took it for granted, that bishops or presbyters would in general be married. "A bishop," says he, "must be blameless, the husband of one wife, having faithful children, not given to riot or unruly." The passage in the epistle to the Corinthians, in which the same apostle speaks of single life, has no bearing whatever on the question of clerical celibacy. It was not to the clergy, but to the Corinthians in general that he wrote; and it was not a general rule that he laid down; but an advice as to how Christians ought to act in the *then* afflictive circumstances of the Christian church. "I suppose," said he, "that this is good for the *present distress.*" Many, indeed, very early perverted his language to a purpose very different from his meaning; and an undue importance was attached to celibacy and virginity; but many generations passed away before any stringent *laws* were made on the subject. We learn from Eusebius, that the *example of the apostles* was regarded by the general church in the fourth century, as the most decisive argument against the heretics, who repudiated matrimony. "Clemens," says Eusebius, approvingly, "recited the *apostles who lived in wedlock*, against those who reject marriage, saying, *What! do they condemn* *the apostles?* for Peter and Philip employed their industry in the bringing up of their children."* Jerome admits that married men were, in his time, more frequently elected bishops, than those who were single; and Socrates mentions it as a *remarkable* custom, which he had found to prevail in Thessaly, but no where else, that presbyters who, after receiving ordination, still continued to live with their wives, were deposed from the ministry. "The author and ringleader of that custom in Thessaly," says he, "was Theodorus, a presbyter of Triva, a city of that country, the writer of those wanton and amorous books which he made in the prime of his flourishing youth, and entitled, Æthiopica."† It is instructive to know, that he who first introduced the absolute prohibition of the marriage of the clergy was one whose own character was so indifferent in his youth. It is easy and natural, from the extreme of licentiousness on the one hand, to pass to the extreme of rigid, self-

* Euseb. Hist. Eccles., lib. iii. cap. 27.

† Socrat. Scholast. Hist., lib. v. cap. 21.

righteous austerity, on the other. Such was the beginning of *enforced* clerical celibacy. It is well ascertained, however, that the clergy in general were married, at least till the beginning of the seventh century; and it was not till the pontificate of Gregory VII., the famous Hildebrand, in the eleventh, that chaste and holy matrimony was utterly banished from the priesthood even of the Church of Rome. And now Rome stands alone among the churches of Christendom, for the rigour with which celibacy is enforced on her priests. In her, then, undeniably do we find this other mark of the apostacy, "forbidding to marry." The last mark,

4. "Commanding to abstain from meats," is equally descriptive of Popery. During the apostolic age itself, there were not a few at Rome, as we learn from the epistle to the Roman church, who looked upon it as unlawful to eat certain meats. "One believeth that he may eat all things; another who is weak eateth herbs." So long as those who scrupled on this subject, regulated only their own conduct by

their own light, sought merely to maintain a conscience void of offence, and presumed not to infringe on the liberty of their fellow-Christians, there might be inconvenience, but there was no serious or fatal error. Both parties might live together in peace and mutual charity, and both might be accepted of God. The injunction to both was, "Let not him that eateth despise him that eateth not; and let not him which eateth not judge him that eateth; for God hath received him."* Had this rule been faithfully observed, all would have gone well. But many to whom the apostle wrote, were not content with the admonitions of heavenly wisdom. They were not willing to receive the gospel in its simplicity. They were bent on establishing their own righteousness. They hoped by austerities to recommend themselves to God's favour; and they laboured with all their might to bring the church again into bondage to "the rudiments of the world." This spirit was manifested in many different parts of the Christian church;

* Rom. xiv. 3.

and wherever it appeared, the Christians were enjoined to resist it; to "let no man judge them in respect of meat or drink," but "to stand fast in the liberty wherewith Christ had made them free." In the epistle to the Colossians, Paul denounces, as led astray "by philosophy and vain deceit," and as teaching "commandments and doctrines of men," those who, under a "show of wisdom in will-worship, and humility and neglecting of the body,"* endeavoured to infringe upon the liberty of the Christians in this matter. For a while the self-righteous teachers, who insisted on the religious duty of abstinence from meats, were classed with decided heretics. In course of time, however, the little leaven leavened the general lump; and for centuries past the Church of Rome has adopted and systematized the pestilent heresy, which the Spirit of God so clearly denounced. The Church of Rome "commands" all her votaries "to abstain from meats," from flesh, butter, and the like, on Fri-

* Col. ii. 8, 23.

days, Saturdays, ember weeks, vigils, and the whole of Lent. The moral commandments of God are not half so strictly enforced or observed in that corrupt Church, as this commandment of men. A dispensation indeed may be *purchased;* but without that, it is sacrilege in such cases to eat meat. Popery teaches, that to steal small sums,* to lie in matters that do not "*greatly* dishonour God, or "*notably* prejudice our neighbour," are only *venial* sins,† but that it is a *mortal* sin to eat meat on Fridays or Saturdays.‡§ Men are thus encouraged in sin, and at the same time bound in abject bondage to the priests. How galling is this bondage, is attested from his own experience, by Blanco White, himself formerly a Popish priest in Spain. "It is Friday," says he, describing the life of a Spanish Papist: "it is Friday, a

* Bailly's Moral Theology, vol. ii. p. 282.

† Dr Doyle's Catechism. ‡ Butler's Catechism, p. 53.

§ By a late dispensation of the Pope, the obligation of fasting on *Saturdays* is taken away in Britain. This grace is, no doubt, intended to smooth the way for the reconversion of this country.

day of penance: he has made but one meal and that on fish; had he tasted meat, he feels assured, that he should have *subjected himself to the pains of hell.*" Thus does the Church of Rome "command to abstain from meats." Join this then to the other marks which we have already considered, and it must be manifest, that in Rome we find that apostacy, which was to be characterized by the worship of "demons," or the canonized spirits of the departed, by "speaking lies in hypocrisy, forbidding to marry, and commanding to abstain from meats."

CHAPTER II.

The Adversary of Christ.

2 THESSALONIANS ii. 3.

And that Man of sin be revealed, the Son of perdition, who opposeth, (or more properly, "the Adversary.)*

THIS apostacy was to have a recognized head. When the apostacy was fairly developed, then was the Man of sin to be revealed; then was the Son of perdition, and the Adversary, to appear. Who is this Man of sin, this Son of perdition, this Adversary? He can be none other than the Pope, not meaning, of course, this or that particular Pope, but the succession of Popes, regarded as one, just as the several sovereigns of the four great monarchies of Daniel, though

* Ὁ ἀντικείμενος.

consisting of many successive individuals, are spoken of as only "four kings." And the title of "Man of sin" is most descriptive, whether we regard the general character of the Popes, or the relation in which they have stood to that corrupt system of lies and priestcraft, of which they have formed the corner-stone. The Popes have, in their own lives, been the embodiment of wickedness. So notorious has been their depravity, that even Genebrard and Cardinal Baronius, the advocates of the Papacy, have been obliged to confess, that for about 150 years at least, the several heads of the church were "monsters of wickedness," and might more justly be called "apostates than apostles."* Some have had more regard to appearances than others; but in all cases, their power, their influence, their energy, have all been exerted in fostering irreligion and iniquity. The Pope is, in true and proper sense, the antichrist, the adversary of God and godliness. It is vain for Papists, and their partizans among professing Protestants, to say, that "the Ad-

* Geneb. iv. p. 552. Baron. Ann. 912. Paris, 1744.

versary," here foretold by Paul, or the antichrist of John, must be an open and avowed infidel, making war upon every thing that has the *appearance* of religion, and therefore not to be identified with the Pope, who makes large professions of religion. It is plain, from the way in which the Antichrist is spoken of by John, that *he* attached no such idea to that character. "Little children," says he, referrring to the approaching desolation of Jerusalem, "it is the last hour;* and as ye have heard that the antichrist shall come, even now are there many antichrists; whereby we know that it is the last hour."† There is here an obvious allusion to the signs, which our Lord had given, by which his disciples might know that the desolation of Jerusalem was nigh. "Take heed," said the Lord Jesus, "that no man deceive you; for many shall come in *my name*, saying, I am Christ, and shall deceive many." "There shall arise *false Christs* and false prophets, and shall show great signs and wonders; in so much, that, if

* Ἡ ἐσχάτη ὥρα· † 1 John ii. 18.

it were possible, they shall deceive the very elect."* The "many antichrists" then, of whom the beloved disciple speaks, as having already appeared, instead of being avowed enemies of Christ, on the contrary, assumed his character, and laid claim to the honours which were due to him alone. Of course, when THE Antichrist should appear, he would appear in the same character; not as the professed enemy of Christ, but as "*coming in his name.*"† Such is John's Antichrist. The Man of sin, the Adversary, in the passage before us, is exactly of the same description. He is an enemy indeed, but an enemy in disguise. The name of Judas Iscariot, "the Son of perdition," bestowed upon him, points him out as a disciple, but a traitorous one; and the position which we shall find him occupying "in the temple of God" cuts up by the roots the idea of an avowedly atheis-

* Matthew xxiv. 5.

† The early Christians understood this well. Lactantius, for instance, speaking of Antichrist, says, "He shall feign himself *to be Christ*, and shall fight against the truth." Lib. vii. sect. 19, p. 499, Lugd. Bat. 1652.

tic or infidel antichrist.* Now the Pope answers exactly to the character of the Adversary,—the enemy of God, in whatever light we view that system, which he controls and governs. The grand cardinal principles of Christianity, have been beautifully and comprehensively summed up by Merle D'Aubigné, under the three heads—the word of God alone—the grace of Christ alone—the work of the Spirit alone. To each and all of these, the Pope is diametrically "opposed."

I. He "opposes" the word of God. In all ages he has done what he could to keep it out of the hands of the people. For centuries he kept it locked up in a language which the laity could not understand. The Reformation has made it impossible for him to keep all translations of it out of the hands of his vassals as effectually as before; but his enmity against the circulation of the Scriptures has been only the more clearly developed thereby. Witness the Bible burning by his priests in Ireland, in Madeira, and in

* See note D.

every place, where he has the power. Witness the bull of Pope Pius VII. issued in 1816, in which the Bible Society is denounced as "this pestilence," "this defilement of the faith so imminently dangerous to souls." But perhaps this enmity was excited only by the false and corrupt translations of the heretics? No. Bibles printed in Italy, even from *Popish versions*, but without note or comment, are equally prohibited under the severest penalties. And even as to Bibles, well fortified with notes, their *general* circulation is absolutely forbidden. In accordance with the regulations of the Council of Trent, the fourth rule of the Congregation of the Index prohibits the reading of the Bible in any case without an express *licence* from the bishop with the advice of the priest or confessor; and provides that "if any one shall have the presumption to read or possess it, *without written permission*, he shall not receive absolution, until he shall have first delivered up such Bible to the ordinary."* This rule is binding at this hour.

* De Libris Prohibitis, Concil. Trid. p. 231, Lipsiæ, 1842.

In the Encyclical letter of Pope Gregory, published in 1844, that Pontiff, after referring to this and many other prohibitory enactments of the church on the subject, expressly ratifies them in the following terms: "Moreover we confirm and renew the decrees recited above, delivered in former times by apostolic authority, *against the publication, distribution, reading, and possession of books of the Holy Scriptures translated into the vulgar tongue.*" His Holiness treats the opinion of the Jansenists as to "the holy books being useful at all times, and for all the faithful" as an "exploded" heresy; and calls upon the bishops to take care that the reading of them be permitted to *none*," but "such as it might be deemed necessary to *confirm* in faith and piety."* To the

* There are few indeed whom Popish priests would hope to "*confirm* in the faith" by the reading of the Bible. Almost all the priests we ever heard of seem to be exactly of the mind of Richard du Mans, who at Trent gave it as his opinion that the reading of the Scriptures ought not to be encouraged, "*as the Lutherans only gained those that read them.*" In this country the laws of Trent are not so strictly *enforced* on this subject as elsewhere; but this is merely from motives of expediency, not because the priests in this country disapprove them. Every Popish priest

vast mass of the people this amounts to neither more nor less than an absolute prohibition. In making such prohibitions the Pope and his prelates sometimes affect great respect and reverence for the word of God. When Archbishops Troy and Murray, for instance, and the Popish clergy of Dublin, found, in 1820, that "the Scriptures, with or without note or comment, were unfit to be used as a school-book," their champion* in the Kildare Place Society defended them on the ground that it was intolerable that so holy a book should be "thumbed by every child in the school!" When it suits his purpose Antichrist can speak with great veneration of the Bible. But the general language of the Pope's most famous doctors runs in a very different style. In the Council of Trent the prelates spoke of the Bible as "dead ink," an inanimate dumb thing, and the "black gospel." When they speak honestly, the traditions of

is SWORN to uphold ALL the decrees and decisions of Trent, which are of unquestionable authority throughout the whole Roman Catholic church.

* Mr O'Connell.

men are far preferred before it. "Tradition," says Cardinal Baronius, "is the foundation of the Scriptures, and excels them in this, that the Scriptures cannot subsist unless they be strengthened by tradition; but tradition hath strength enough without the Scriptures."* This shows no great respect for the Scriptures; but Linden speaks of them with positive contempt. "Traditions," says he, "are the most certain foundations of faith, the most sure ground of the Scriptures, the impenetrable buckler of Ajax, the suppressor of all heresies. On the other side, the Scripture is a nose-of-wax, a dead and killing letter without life, a mere shell without a kernel, a leaden rule, a wood of thieves, a shop of heretics."† What infidel could speak more blasphemously of the word of God; that word which all true Christians feel in their experience to be more to be desired than gold, yea, than much fine gold, sweeter also than honey and the honeycomb. Not so did those Fathers

* Baron. Ann. tom. i. sect. 11, p. 454, Col. Agrip. 1609.
† Lind. Panopl. lib. i. chap. 22.

speak of it, to whom the Papists are so fond of appealing. "Hear me," says Chrysostom, "ye men of the world. Get ye the BIBLE, that most wholesome remedy for the soul; if ye will nothing else, yet at the least get the New Testament, St Paul's Epistles, the Gospels, and the Acts, that they may be your constant and earnest teachers."* These men apprehended no danger from its wide and profuse circulation. "Here we are taught," says Jerome, (expounding the words of the apostle, "Let the word of Christ dwell in you richly")—"here we are taught that the lay-people ought to have the word of God, not only sufficiently, but also with abundance, that they may teach and counsel one another." And the necessity of tradition they not only did not admit, but directly repudiated. "If this be not *written*," says Tertullian, rejecting the error of Hermogenes about the eternity of matter, "let Hermogenes fear the woe which belongs to them who add or detract."† "As we deny not

* Chrys. Opera. Homil. ix. tom. xi. p. 391. Paris, 1734.

† Tertull. contra Herm. cap. 22, tom. ii. p. 308. Wirceburg: 1781.

that which is *written*," says Jerome to Helvidius, "so we refuse those things which are *not written*. Every thing that we assert we must show from the Holy Scripture." "I require the voice of the shepherd," says Augustine; "*read* this matter out of the prophets; read it to me out of the psalms; read it me out of the law; read it me out of the gospel; read it out of the apostles."* If there ever could have been any plea for the authority of tradition, it must have been in the early ages of the church; but so long as the true light remained in the church, the *only* appeal was "to the law and to the testimony." Why does the Pope, in opposition to those fathers, of whom he boasts, show so much enmity to the Bible, and labour so hard to suppress it? The reason is not far to seek. The Bible is against *him* as much as *he* is against the Bible; and some of the authorities of Rome have even had the simplicity to confess so much. "Many points of doctrine," says Andradius, "would reel and totter if they were not sup-

* Augustini Opera. tom. iv. lib. i. c. 35.

ported by the help of tradition." And said Pope Paul V., "The Scripture is a book, which if any man will keep close to, he will quite ruin the Catholic faith."* The "Catholic faith" must at all hazards be upheld, and therefore the word of God must be made void by his traditions. He takes away the key of knowledge from the people. He neither enters in himself; and them that would enter in he hinders.† But does not this prove that he is the "Adversary?"

II. The Pope "opposes" the grace of our Lord Jesus Christ. There is nothing more clearly revealed in the word of God than that all our hopes of acceptance and salvation are founded on the mere mercy and grace of God, and that that mercy and grace come to us solely through

* Zouch's Walton's Lives. Life of Donne, vol. i. p. 138.

† It was a striking and characteristic proof of the enmity of Rome against God's word, that when Clement Marot's version of the Psal· s was beginning to be commonly sung in the court of Francis I., the Cardinal of Lorraine caused the impure and licentious odes of Horace to be translated into French verse, in order that they might supplant it!!

the finished work of Immanuel the Lord our Righteousness. The whole doctrine of the papacy is directly subversive of this grand "article of a standing, or a falling church." The grace of the Gospel and the doctrine of Rome on this subject, are mutually destructive of each other. This the Popish priests know well. This has even been admitted by some of them in the most affecting circumstances. Stephen Gardiner, Bishop of Winchester, the murderer of Latimer and Ridley, on his death-bed gave a striking proof of his strong sense of this. In his last illness, with which he was smitten on the very day that these martyrs were burned, he was affected with great horror of conscience, and with dreadful forebodings in the prospect of death. In his distress he often exclaimed, "*Erravi cum Petro; sed non flevi cum Petro,*" "I have erred with Peter, but I have not wept like him."* Dr Davy, bishop of Chichester, seeing Gardiner's dreadful state, and feeling that the juggleries of Popery could afford no support at

* Wrangham's British Plutarch.

such an hour, endeavoured to comfort him with the offers of free justification through the blood of Christ, as contained in the Scripture. How did the dying man receive his friendly counsels? Convinced, but not changed, he showed the natural enmity of the heart of man against the doctrines of grace. "What, my Lord," cried Gardiner, "will you open that gap now? Then farewell all together. To me, and such other in my case, indeed you may speak it; *but open this window to the people, and then farewell all together.*"* And the testimony of Gardiner is true. Let only this doctrine of justification by faith alone have free course among the people, and then farewell to the superstitions of Rome altogether. It was through this that Luther gave such a deadly wound to the papacy. *Without* this all the enthusiasm of John Ronge will come to nothing.

In two essential respects does Rome pour contempt on the grace of our Lord Jesus Christ. On the one hand, it teaches that man has no

* Life of Ridley.

such *need* of the grace of Christ as the Bible declares; and on the other, it vilifies and degrades that perfect righteousness of his, in virtue of which the grace of God is extended. Popery completely neutralises the *need* of Christ's grace, by its doctrine as to human merits. It does not indeed in so many words deny the grace of Christ; but by flattering the pride of man, by representing him as in part at least his own Saviour, and as able to *deserve* salvation at God's hands, it makes that grace an empty name. "If any one shall say," decrees the Council of Trent, "that a justified person does not *truly merit*, ... eternal life, let him be accursed."* He that believes himself "*truly to merit eternal life*," can have no conception of being indebted to *grace*. He must have something in himself whereof to glory; his own works must be the ground and foundation of his hopes. It is nothing to say, that such an one, trusts in Christ as *well* as his own works. Christ must be all to

* Sess. vi. De Justifica. Canon xxxii. p. 38. Lipsiæ, 1842.

us, or he will be nothing. The Galatians tried to join Christ and the works of the law together in the matter of justification. But what said the apostle to them? "If ye are justified by the law, ye are fallen from grace." The divine plan of justification altogether excludes the works of the law. "To him that worketh not, but believeth on Him that justifieth the ungodly, his faith is counted for righteousness."* "Therefore," says Paul in another place, "we conclude that a man is *justified by faith without the deeds of the law.*" Such is God's way of justifying a sinner, that the most wicked may be encouraged to come to Him, that "boasting may be excluded," that all idea of human *merits* may be rooted out, that "no flesh may glory in his presence." The Pope's way of justification is the very reverse. "If any man," say his prelates at Trent, "shall affirm, that justifying faith is nothing else than dependence on the mercy of God, for remission of sins for Christ's

* Rom. iv. 6.

sake, or that *it is by faith alone that we are justified*, let him be accursed."*

The doctrine of free salvation is too humbling a doctrine for those who go about to establish their own righteousness, and who wish to *merit* eternal life. The whole doctrine of popery, on the other hand, is fitted to minister to the pride and self-sufficiency of the natural mind, and that in the grossest manner. It not merely represents man as able to merit for himself, and to "make some atonement to God by his own voluntary sufferings" for his *own* sins; but it goes the blasphemous length of maintaining, that men, who are "conceived in sin and shapen in iniquity," and in "whose flesh dwelleth no good thing," may do much more than the law requires, and thus by works of supererogation," work out a righteousness available not only for themselves, but also for the salvation of others. "In this respect," says the catechism of the Council of Trent, "is the supreme goodness of God worthy of the highest praises and thanks-

* Sess. vi, can. xii. p. 36.

givings that he hath granted this unto human infirmity, that one man may be able *to satisfy for another.**" Were this indeed the case, where, we ask, had been the need that the Son of the Highest should leave the bosom of the Father, and submit to the accursed death of the cross? If one sinner can in any sense satisfy divine justice for his fellow-sinner, then verily "Christ hath died in vain." But there is not a trace of any such doctrine in the Bible; but much expressly to the contrary. The holiest of God's saints have ever had to confess with David, "If thou, O Lord, shouldst mark iniquity, who, O Lord, should stand?" "When ye have done all," said our Lord himself, say "We are unprofitable servants; we have done what it was our duty to do." He that inculcates such a doctrine as this propagates "another gospel, which is not another," and deludes the souls of men. But what then? The interests of the papacy are advanced, and that is enough to cover any iniquity. The superabundant merits of the saints

* Catechism, part ii. c. 5, p. 257.

form "a sort of bank," says De la Hogue,* out of which pardons and indulgences may be dispensed to those of the faithful, whose merits are deficient. The Pope holds the keys of "the celestial treasury;" and through the belief in this figment, the see of St Peter is aggrandized. Is this an exploded delusion of the dark ages? No. In the present day, the doctrine has been openly and boldly proclaimed. In 1824, Pope Leo XII. issued a bull for the observance of a jubilee, in which peculiar privileges were offered to the faithful, who should make a pilgrimage to Rome. Listen to the blasphemous language in which the sovereign pontiff announced to his children throughout Christendom, his kind intentions in regard to them. "We have resolved," said he, "in virtue of the authority given to us by Heaven, fully to unlock that sacred treasure composed of the merits, sufferings, and virtues of Christ our Lord, and of his virgin-mother, and of all saints, which the Author

* De Penitentia, p. 334. Dub. 1825.

of human salvation has entrusted to our dispensation." *

Such are the unblushing pretensions of the Papacy at this day; and thus are souls who confide in them deceived to their eternal ruin. The gospel of the grace of God makes sin appear to be, as it is indeed, exceeding sinful, and sinks the pardoned sinner in the dust before God. The doctrine of Rome makes sin appear a mere trifle for which man himself can atone, and puffs up wretched sinners with insufferable pride. Witness the epitaph which Boccaccio, whose life was mostly spent in pandering to the basest passions of the licentious mind, after atoning for his sins by the penances of his old age, ordered to be inscribed on his tombstone: —"Under this pile lie the ashes and bones of John Boccaccio. His soul sits before the throne of God, adorned with the *merits* of his life."† Witness the following inscription engraved on a monument erected only in 1819 in one

* Glasgow Lectures.

† Men of Modern Times. Article Boccaccio.

of the Popish chapels in Cork:—"I. H. S. Sacred to the memory of the benevolent Edward Molloy, the friend of humanity and father of the poor. He employed the wealth of this world only to secure the riches of the next, and leaving a *balance of merit* on the book of life, he made heaven *debtor* to mercy."* What can be more blasphemous? But such is the genuine fruit of the doctrine inculcated by the Pope and the Council of Trent, that sinful man can "truly *merit* eternal life."

But while the Popish doctrine of justification is thus fitted to lull men asleep in their sins, it is equally derogatory to the righteousness of Christ. If those who believe in Jesus *need* in any respect to satisfy divine justice for themselves, if they *need* the merit of any saint or any creature whatever to gain pardon and acceptance with God, the redemption of Christ must have been incomplete, his righteousness cannot be a perfect righteousness, his atonement has not "magnified the law and made it ho-

† Protestant, vol. ii. p. 3.

nourable." Thus is the glorious work of Christ degraded that the merits of men may be exalted. And the sacrifice of the mass, which Popery has invented, casts additional contempt on the atoning sacrifice of the one great High Priest. It is expressly declared by Paul that the perfection of Christ's sacrifice, as contradistinguished from the sacrifices under the law, was manifested by this, that it was "once" and *only* "once" offered; and that after that offering, "once for all," there was need of "no more offering for sin." "Every priest," says he, referring to the Jewish worship, "standeth daily ministering and offering oftentimes the same sacrifices, which can never take away sin; but this Man, after he had offered ONE sacrifice for sin, for ever sat down on the right hand of God, from henceforth expecting till his enemies be made his footstool. For by ONE OFFERING he hath for ever perfected them that are sanctified." Now the doctrine of the mass is diametrically opposed to the inspired Apostle. In the Creed of Pope Pius IV., which every popish priest is sworn to maintain, it is thus declared, "I profess likewise, that in the mass, there is offered to God, a true, proper, and propitiatory sacrifice for the sins of the living and the dead."* Thus, by the pretended *repetition* of that sacrifice, which was offered "once for all," does Popery directly impugn the efficacy of our Lord's finished work and perfect atonement.

This is enough to show how utterly opposed is popery to the gospel. But add to all this, that in the Pope's church, no spiritual benefit whatever can be had without the payment of money, and it will be seen still more clearly how directly he "opposes the *grace* of our Lord Jesus Christ. "Ho every one that thirsteth," saith the Saviour, "come ye to the waters, and he that hath no money, come, buy and eat, yea, buy wine and milk without money and without price." No, saith the Pope, no grace, no mercy, no pardon, no spiritual privilege, but for those who can pay for them. He has directly reversed

* Bulla Pii IV. apud canon. et decret. sacrosanct. concil. Triden. p. 226. Lipsiae, 1842.

the saying of our Lord, "How hardly shall they that are *rich* enter into the kingdom of heaven." According to the doctrine and practice of Rome, it is "How hardly shall the *poor* enter into the kingdom." He that can give or bequeath money enough to buy masses for his soul, cannot fail to enter into heaven's bliss; but as for the poor and the destitute, who have nothing to give, woe to them; there are no merits of the saints, no masses for *them;* they must suffer for themselves for ages in purgatory fire.* In what a light does this represent the Pope and his clergy! They believe or profess to believe, that souls are agonizing in that place of torment; they assert the possession of full power to deliver them from the state of woe, and introduce them into all the glory and happiness of heaven; and yet, unless they are specially paid for it, they will not

* In the "Tax Tables of the Apostolic Chancery," published by Papal authority, in which a regular price is fixed for the pardon of all sorts of sins, however atrocious, the following intimation occurs:—"Note diligently, that these graces *are not granted to the poor,* because they have not wherewithal that they may be comforted."—Cobbin's Book of Popery, p. 43.

breathe a prayer, they will not offer a mass, they will not lift their little finger for their relief. Thus do they make merchandise of men's souls. The astonishing thing is that the people should submit to their extortions; that they can be led to believe that the "gift of God can be purchased with money." Now, can there be a doubt, that he who maintains and upholds such a system is "the Adversary" of God and every thing that is good?

III. The Pope "opposes" the work of the Holy Spirit. Christianity teaches that all that is good in man comes solely and entirely from the working of the Holy Ghost. It tells us that so deep and desperate is the corruption of the natural heart, that except a man be born again, except he be "created in Christ Jesus unto good works," except he be "renewed in the very spirit of his mind," he can never enter into the kingdom of God. This new birth, this new creation, comes only from the Spirit of God. "That which is born of the flesh is flesh: that which is born of the Spirit is spirit." The true Christian is both "born of the Spirit" and "led by the Spirit," and kept by the Spirit through faith unto eternal life. It is the Spirit of God alone that "works in him both to will and to do of his good pleasure." It is the Spirit that enables him to hold fellowship with God in his worship; and without that Spirit "he can do nothing." Now to all this Popery is utterly opposed. The Jansenists of France at one time attempted to introduce the true doctrine of God's word on this vital subject into the Church of Rome. They taught, that the grace of the Spirit of Christ, "the efficacious principle of every kind of good, is necessary to every good work; that without it, not only nothing is done, but likewise nothing *can* be done." * How did the occupant of St Peter's chair treat their efforts? He fulminated against them the famous bull *Unigenitus;* he denounced them as little better than heretics, and condemned the proposition, with

* Quesnell, Abrege de la Morale de l'Evangile, Joan xv. v. 5, Paris, 1693.

many others equally scriptural, as "false, captious, shocking, offensive to pious ears, scandalous, pernicious, blasphemous," &c.† The Pope cannot endure the truth of God's word on this subject. He knows, that it would subvert the whole of that system of superstition, by which he deludes men's souls. If Papists believed that without the blessing of God's free and sovereign Spirit, no spiritual benefit could be conferred on them, they would not prize as they do those privileges, which they imagine the priests of Rome capable of conferring. They are taught to trust in their priests, as having full powers both to make them Christians and to keep them so. The sacraments in their hands are represented as having a magical efficacy, and operating upon those who receive them exactly like a charm. "A sacrament," says Bishop Hay, "is an outward sensible action, or sacred sign, ordained of Jesus Christ, as a *sure and certain means* of bringing grace into our souls." Although God has expressly reserved in his own

† Bulla Clem. XI. ap. can. et Decret. Concil. Trid. p. 291.

hands the power either to give or withhold his blessing from his own ordinances, according to his sovereign pleasure—although Christ hath declared, that it is the Spirit that quickeneth—that the flesh, or any outward ordinance, of itself profiteth nothing,—the poor deluded Papists are taught to believe, that the sacraments, if *duly administered* by Romish priests, have a power *in themselves* to "confer grace" upon those who receive them. "If any one shall say," says the Council of Trent, "that by the sacraments grace is not conferred *ex opere operato*, (*i.e.* by the mere celebration and reception of them), let him be anathema."* In virtue of this doctrine, every child, without exception, that has received the sacrament of baptism, is taught to regard himself as indubitably "a child of God—a disciple of Jesus Christ—the temple of God, who dwells in him by his grace."† Although it be ever so manifest by their lives, that hundreds of such baptized ones

* Sess. vii., Can. 8, de Sacram. p. 43.

† Catechism of W. E. Andrews, recommended by Dr Milner.

are still the children of the devil, it would be heresy to question their regeneration—to hint, that, like Nicodemus, they still need "to be born again." The divine life has beyond question been commenced in their souls, and all that they need for the maintenance and perfection of that life, is only to avail themselves of the other sacraments of the church, to confess their sins duly to the priest, to receive extreme unction at last, and without doubt they shall be finally saved.

What absurdity can be greater, more unscriptural, or more irrational than this theory of necessary sacramental regeneration? Take an individual instance, as an illustration of its character. In the time of Louis, the son of Charlemagne, the Norwegian sea-kings sadly infested the coast of France. The garrisons and flotillas established by the father no longer giving protection from their depredations, the son tried to secure himself and his people by a more effectual plan. He set to work to make them Christians; he prevailed on some of them to be baptised; and, by way of inducement, presented each of them with a suit of white, in which he might appear at the font, and which thereafter became his own. One Easter, it happened that the number of these converts was unusually great. The white robes provided for them were exhausted; and, in the extremity, some linen belonging to the clergy was hastily made up for the purpose. This moved the choler of one of these northern barbarians, when he was offered an inferior robe. He protested, "that he had already come twenty times to be baptized,—that he had always received the best white robes; but as they now put him off with a garment only fit for a herdsman, he disclaimed their Christianity"!* Now this man was duly and canonically baptized: this man of course had become a new creature; and such was his Christianity. Papists, when hard pressed with such a case, have their salvos and distinctions. They tell us of an "*obstacle*" in the state of the man's own mind, which might prevent

* Britons and Saxons, p. 73.

the "supernatural virtue" of the sacrament from *taking effect;* whereas, say they, no such "obstacle" can be found in the case of infants, who have no actual sin to *resist* the sacramental grace of baptism. But this is obviously a mere subterfuge. The whole of their devotions and religious services are pervaded and vitiated by the same principle. If "the work be done," if the task be performed, if the beads be duly counted, if the prescribed prayers be said, if the crossing of themselves, the sprinkling with holy water, the genuflexions, the beating of their breasts, be gone through, they are led to believe that all is right,—that the state of the heart is a matter of no moment. Popish priests may attempt to elude the charge; but the fact that the most essential parts of their public service are conducted in Latin, in a language which not one in a hundred of their people can understand, proves to demonstration that the maxim on which they proceed is still, as of old, that "ignorance is the mother of devotion," and that "bodily service" is every thing. Thus the grand end for which religious services were appointed, viz. that man might have fellowship with his Maker, is clean subverted. Although reason as well as Scripture declares that God is a Spirit, and that they who worship him must worship him in spirit and in truth, the devotees of Rome are encouraged to believe the very reverse. Instead, therefore, of their religion bringing them nearer to God, it is the very means of keeping them at a distance from Him, and deluding them to their everlasting ruin.

While popery is thus subversive of all spiritual religion, it is of necessity equally ruinous to the *morality* of its votaries. Individual Roman Catholics may be found distinguished for the purity and blamelessness of their lives; but this is not in consequence of, but in spite of their religion. The belief instilled into them that the mere reception of sacraments confers grace, and makes them Christians, must have the most pernicious effects on the lives and character of the mass of that communion. They must be led to entertain views of Christian character essentially different from those laid down in the Bible, and so be hardened in sin. In point of fact, it is manifest from the whole history of popery, that immorality and wickedness of the most flagrant kind do not in the least invalidate the Christian character of its adherents, provided they are only submissive to the church. It is well known that Charles II., who lived a life of debauchery to the last, was hailed as an honour to the Church of Rome, when, without giving the least evidence of genuine repentance, he avowed his attachment to popery on his death-bed. Louis XIV. of France was not the less regarded by that church, as "the Most Christian King," because of his well-known profligacy. The banditti in Italy itself have their confessors; and the public harlots of Rome are admitted to all the privileges of the church. Nay, to such a pitch of wickedness has popery advanced, that in the "holy city," communion with the church has even been required as a *qualification* before a woman could be allowed to practise as a harlot. "It is known," says a writer of the 17th century, quoted by Macgavin, "that the pope authorises and protects public stews, in order to draw a considerable revenue from them; but it is not universally known, that to advance the reputation of that crime, which, indeed, is not accounted any by the Court of Rome, the popes will not suffer any women to prostitute themselves, unless they be *Christians;* and, therefore, by order of his holiness, Jewish, Pagan, and Mahometan women, who have a mind to set up that trade at Rome, must first be baptised."* How truly has the Spirit of God characterized the apostate church as "Babylon the great, the Mother of harlots, and abominations of the earth!"

Such is the wickedness naturally flowing from the popish doctrine of sacramental efficacy; but the way in which that sacramental efficacy is *communicated* to the elements, shows still more the daring impiety of the system. It has been already stated, that these have a power

* Protestant, vol. I. p. 45.

in *themselves* to confer grace, if *duly celebrated.* Now, the due celebration of the sacraments depends essentially on "*the intention*" of the priest. "Without *intention* in the priest, there is no real sacrament. If the priest *intend* to bless, the people are blessed! If the priest intend not to bless, they are not blessed!"* Such is the doctrine of Rome, first formally established in the Council of Florence, and confirmed by those which have succeeded. The object of it is plainly to vest all spiritual power in the hands of the priests, to make the people crouch at their feet, and to seek by all means to propitiate their favour. Thus the clergy are every thing; and God's Holy Spirit, whose prerogative it is alone to bless the ordinances of God, is contemned and degraded.

Now, when we see that the pope thus directly and systematically sets himself in opposition to the word of God, the grace of Christ, and the work of the Holy Ghost, is it possible any longer to doubt that he is indeed the Man of Sin, the adversary of God and godliness.

* Rogers' Antipopery, sec. xvii. p. 237.

CHAPTER III.

The Rival Christ.

2 Thessalonians ii. 4.

"And exalteth himself above all that is called God, or that is worshipped; so that he, as God, sitteth in the temple of God, shewing himself that he is God."

We have seen the irreligion, the unholiness of that system of superstition of which the Pope is the head, and its *utter contrariety* to the doctrine of Christ. We come now more particularly to consider the arrogant assumptions and blasphemous pretensions of the Papacy, so clearly depicted in the sure word of prophecy, so many hundred years before it was possible that they could be actually realized. It is here predicted, that the Man of sin would "exalt himself above *all* that is *called* God, or that is worshipped."

The expression is remarkable. It not obscurely indicates, that in the apostate church there would be other objects of worship besides the true God; and we have seen that in the apostate Church of Rome there are "gods many, and lords many," that receive the adorations of their blinded devotees. It implies, moreover, that above both the true God, and all these false objects of worship, the Man of sin would exalt himself. And this is literally the case with the Pope. 1. He exalts himself above the *true* God. He substitutes his own will and traditions for the word and will of God, and requires all to obey them on pain of damnation. Thus is the authority of a mortal man raised above the authority of the Most High God. Nor does he do this only in an indirect way, by claiming for himself the sole and supreme power to *declare* the will of God. We shall see by and by that he sets himself above the Highest, by asserting the right to dispense with the acknowledged law of God, to abrogate and annul *it.** 2. He ex-

* See Chapter V. The Lawless One.

alts himself above all that is *called* God. Whenever creatures are joined as objects of worship with the Creator, the latter is invariably found to occupy an inferior place in the esteem of the worshippers, to the former. We have seen, for instance, that the Virgin Mary ranks much higher in the Church of Rome than God himself. Yet above both the Virgin and all other objects of idolatry the Pope is exalted. A Papist is encouraged to "appeal from the court of God's justice, to the court of his Mother's mercy;" but no appeal is permitted from the judgment of the Pope. His sentence is supreme, his award is final, and cannot be reversed. And accordingly Stephen, Archbishop of Patraca, declared, with the approbation of the fifth Lateran Council, that the Pope possessed "power above all powers, both in heaven and in earth."*

Now, when such are the pretensions of the Papacy, it need be no matter of surprise that it should be predicted of the Man of sin, that he, "as God, should sit in the temple of God, shew-

* Labb. Concil., tom. xiv. p. 269. Lutet. 1672.

ing himself that he is God." The Pope exhibits himself to the church, as "God upon earth." It is this especially that constitutes him "the Antichrist." The Antipopes, that appeared from time to time in the Papal church, were not professed enemies of the Papacy, but rival Popes. And just so the Antichrist is "*the Rival Christ*," usurping his throne, and claiming his honours.

Sitting in the "central chair of unity," the Pope lays claim to the incommunicable prerogatives of God, and even calls himself by his names. In various ways does he usurp the essential prerogatives of the Most High.

1. He takes to himself the dignity of Universal Bishop, and Head, and Husband of the church. Now Christ is, and can be, the only Head of the church. His headship over the church is founded on his atonement. He loved the church, and gave himself for it; and so he became its Husband and its Head. It was because the blood he shed was the "blood of God," that he purchased it to himself,—that he acquired the right to rule and govern it. None

but he, who is God manifest in the flesh, can exercise the headship over the church. Till the days of Boniface III., who received the title of Universal Bishop or Head of the Church from the Emperor Phocas, the assumption of such a name was accounted, even by the bishops of Rome, as a mark of Antichrist. The testimony of Gregory the Great, only a few years before that event, is very remarkable, and seems to have been ordered by Divine Providence, both to be a standing rebuke to the pride of the Papacy, and to mark the time when the Man of sin was fully revealed. This testimony has been often quoted; but it is too important and appropriate to be omitted here. John, Bishop of Constantinople, had assumed the title; and Gregory, offended, wrote to the Emperor Mauritius to denounce its assumption. "I say it boldly," said he, "whoever either calleth himself Universal Bishop, or desireth so to be called, in the pride of his heart, is the forerunner of Antichrist. . . . . Peter was not called

* Gregor. Opera, lib. vi. Ep. 30. Basil. 1550.

Universal Apostle, and yet my fellow-priest, John, seeks to be called Universal Bishop. *O tempora, O mores!* Europe is exposed a prey to the barbarians, and yet the priests, who should lay themselves in the dust, and weeping roll themselves in ashes, are, in a spirit of vanity, seeking, and boasting themselves in, their new-found and profane titles."* It was only about ten years after this, in 606, that this "new-found and profane title" was transferred from the Bishop of Constantinople to the Bishop of Rome, and ever since it has been borne by the Pope. Thus, then, even on the authority of Pope Gregory, the Pope for the last twelve hundred years has borne the brand of Antichrist.

2. The Pope assumes to be "head over all things to the church," which is the equally incommunicable prerogative of God's eternal Son. This is a power he has asserted again and again; and what is more, to a large extent, so far as this world is concerned, he has exercised it. In virtue of it, he ruled the nations of Christendom

* Gregorii Opera, lib. iv. Ep. 32. See Note E.

for centuries with a rod of iron. How lofty, for instance, are the pretensions of Pope Gregory VII. "The Roman Pontiff," says he, "by right is universal. In him alone is the power of making laws. Let all kings kiss the feet of the Pope. His name alone should be heard in all the churches. It is the only name in this world. It is his right to depose kings. His sentence is to be repealed by no one. It is to be repealed by himself alone."* Thus also, at a later period, wrote Boniface VIII. to Philip the Fair:—"Boniface, Bishop, Servant of the servants of God, to Philip king of France. Fear God, and keep his commandments. We would have you to know, that you are subject to us, both in things spiritual and temporal, and we declare all those to be heretics who believe the contrary. . . . . God hath established us over kings and kingdoms, to pluck up, to overthrow, to scatter, to build, and to plant, in his name, and by his doctrine. Do not allow yourself to be persuaded, that you have not a superior, and that you

* Labbé. Concil. Dict. Pap., tom. x. p. 110.

are not subject to the head of the ecclesiastical hierarchy. He that thinks thus, is a fool; he that obstinately maintains it, is an infidel." Similar pretensions have again and again been advanced by the different Popes; and there were few, in the palmy days of the Papacy, who dared to resist them. Philip the Fair, indeed, did so successfully; and with impunity, in reply to the Pope's insolence, addressed him, as "His Foolishness," instead of "his Holiness." But for the most part the greatest princes had to humble themselves before them. Henry IV. of Germany being excommunicated, and deposed by Hildebrand, had to stand shivering at the gate of the fortress of Canossa for three days in the depth of winter, with bare feet, with head exposed, with only a wretched piece of coarse woollen cloth thrown around him, to cover his nakedness, humbly entreating an audience with the haughty pontiff. At the coronation of the emperor Henry VI., when that monarch stooped to kiss the foot of Pope Celestine, who crowned him, the sovereign pontiff kicked the crown off his head, to show that he had power to take it away, as well as power to bestow it. The humiliation which John, king of England, had to stoop to, is well known, when he had to resign his crown into the hands of the Pope's legate, and humbly to receive it again as a gift from the Holy See; but more potent and high spirited princes have been obliged to submit to as great degradation. In the Royal Hall of the Vatican is to be seen at this day, the picture, in which the heroic Frederick Barbarossa is represented on his knees and elbows before Pope Alexander III., in the public square of Venice. The Pope's foot is on his shoulder; his sceptre is thrown away, and under the picture are these words,—"*Fredericus supplex adorat, fidem et obedientiam pollicitus*:" "Frederick suppliantly adores, promising fidelity and obedience."* These were the times when Popery had the opportunity fully to develope itself; when princes thought it no disgrace to wait as menials at the Pope's table; when the kings of England and of

* Gaussen's Geneva and Rome, p. 11.

France counted it an honour to hold the Pope's stirrups, and to lead his horse by the bridle, one walking at each side of its head; a "sight," says the Contemporary Chronicler, "pleasing to God, to angels, and to men."!*

Such scenes are not enacted at present. The Pope does not find it expedient to obtrude his claim to temporal power over kings and princes. But he has never yet repudiated it; and he never will. Nay, he cannot, without subverting the whole system of superstition and priestcraft, of which he is the head; for his power to dethrone kings is as essential a doctrine of popery, as transubstantiation, or the worship of the Virgin Mary. It is expressly sanctioned by those canons and councils, which *every Roman Catholic priest* is SWORN *to uphold.* The fourth council of the Lateran, in its third canon, enacted formal regulations for the dethronement of refractory kings. The offending sovereign, according to these regulations, "is first to be excommunicated by his metropolitan and suffragans; and if he should

* Sir W. Scott's Tales of a Grandfather. France.

afterward persist in his contumacy for a year, the Roman pontiff, the vicegerent of God, is empowered to degrade him, to absolve his vassals from their fealty, and transfer his dominions to any Catholic who may be able to seize upon them."* The same doctrine was taught and exemplified by the general councils of Lyons and Trent, and five other general councils, whose decisions are universally admitted to be binding in the Romish Church. Yet when the Irish bishops are reminded of this doctrine of their church, they refer us to "their solemn oath" given to the British government, as a proof that they do not hold it. They calculate on the general ignorance that prevails as to the history of their church, and for the most part, their appeal is too successful. But they must not thus be allowed to escape. We ask them how that oath is to be reconciled with the one which they swore to the Pope at consecration? Then, every one of them, in conformity with the bull of Pope Pius IV., swore the following:—"I receive

* Labbé, tom. xi. pars i. p. 148.

and profess ALL that the sacred canons and general councils have delivered, defined, and declared; and I shall endeavour, to the utmost of my power, to cause the same to be held, taught, and preached, to those under my care. This I promise, vow, and swear, so help me God, and these holy Gospels."* By this they are sworn "to hold, teach, and preach" to their own flocks, that very doctrine, on the deposition of heretical princes, sanctioned by the general councils, which, in their oath to the British Government, they have solemnly disowned. Both oaths cannot possibly be taken in good faith. Which has the superior claim on their allegiance, we need be at no loss to determine.

The marked favour shown by the Pontiff, whose ashes are scarcely cold in the grave, for the work of Bellarmine on the Papacy, is of itself demonstrative, that high notions of king-deposing power are the reverse of being peculiar to the dark ages. Gregory XVI. publicly designated Bellarmine as "that most

* Bull. Pii IV., ap. Canon. Con. Trid. p. 227.

excellent defender of the Pontifical prerogatives." Now, what says Bellarmine on this subject? "It is not repugnant to the Gospel," says he, "if in any manner it might be, that the same should be *high priest* of the whole world, and also *emperor* of the whole world." This of course is the *summit* of his wishes; but, in the mean time, he must be content with less. As it is, however, his doctrine is sufficiently high. "The Pope," says the Cardinal, "possesses the power of disposing of the temporal affairs of *all Christians* in *order to their spiritual good.*" And, again,—"The Pope can change kingdoms, and take them away from one, and give them to another, as the highest spiritual prince, if *that be necessary for the salvation of souls.*" Nay, for the promotion of the same object—the spiritual welfare of the true flock—heretical princes and their people are to be devoted to destruction. Here are his own words,—"If, indeed, it can be done, *they are undoubtedly to be extirpated.* But if they cannot, either because they are not sufficiently known, and there is danger, lest the innocent suffer with the guilty; or they are stronger than we, and there is danger, if we attack them in war, that more of us would fall than of them, *then we are to be quiet*."* Now, be it remembered, that this is the doctrine published at Rome with *papal sanction*, no further back than 1842. It is manifest then, that the pretensions of Rome to temporal power, are at this day as arrogant as ever they were, and that she only wants a favourable opportunity to carry them into effect. The fact is, however men may for a purpose disavow the Pope's temporal dominion, it is essentially involved in the all but universally admitted doctrine as to his supremacy. He is not only supreme in all matters spiritual, but he challenges the sole and exclusive right to determine what matters are spiritual, and what are not. In this way he may make any thing spiritual he pleases, and when opportunity shall serve, draw the whole affairs of the world under his absolute control.

3. The Pope lays claim to that infallibility

* Bellarm. Controvers., tom. i.

which is proper to God alone. "It is a sin," say the Decretals, "as great as sacrilege, to reason of any of the Pope's doings."* His doctors assert his infallibility in the strongest terms. "We can believe nothing," says Lewis Capsensis, "unless we believe with divine faith that the Pope is the successor of Peter, and infallible." The assembled cardinals, prelates, and clergy of France, in 1625, declared that "his Holiness was above the reach of calumny, and that his faith was above the reach of error." Harding the Jesuit, in his Confutation of Jewell's Apology, asserts, that "as shepherd of the universal church, in public judgment, in deliberation and definitive sentence, he never erreth, nor ever erred, nor ever can err."† Some Romanists have disputed his infallibility; but the overwhelming weight of authority has been all on the opposite side. The latest Pope, who has pronounced on the subject, has asserted it in the most unqualified manner. "The Pope," says

* Grat. Decret. Distinct. 40.

† Jewell's Defence of the Apology.

Gregory XVI., "is a true monarch; wherefore he ought to be provided with the means necessary for the exercise of his monarchical authority. But the means most necessary to that end must be that which would take away every pretext from his subjects to refuse submission to his decisions and his laws. Now his infallibility alone could have that efficacy; *therefore, the Pope is infallible.*"* Whatever may be thought of this logic, nothing can be more clear or explicit than his Holiness's statement. The infallibility being thus established, he requires, in consequence, implicit and unreasoning faith and obedience. "The Pope," says he, "is supreme head; as such he judges absolutely, and demands the submission of the mind—that is to say, a firm faith in his decisions."† There can be no doubt, then, that papal infallibility is the doctrine of Rome at present, as much as ever it was in the days of Hildebrand. And indeed, to say the truth, those who profess to be Papists, and yet

* The Triumph of the Holy See, by Mauro Capellari (Gregory XVI.), vol. i., p. 145. Louvain, 1834.

† Ibid.

hesitate about the infallibility, are of all men the most inconsistent; for, as has been well remarked, "if the Pope be head of the church, then if he is *not* infallible, without all question he ought to be so."*

4. The Pope claims power to pardon sin. This, too, is peculiar to God; for "who can forgive sins but God alone?" Yet not content with *declaring* pardon to the penitent, he asserts the power to *bestow* forgiveness on whomsoever he pleases.† He pretends to have the key of David, which openeth and no man shutteth, and shutteth and no man openeth, that he can send to heaven or to hell, according as seemeth good in his sight. It was the belief of this power that made the princes of Palermo prostrate themselves at the feet of Martin IV. and address him in the same words as are addressed to Christ himself at the altar: "Thou that takest away the sins of the world have mercy upon us! Thou

* Roger's Antipopery. See Note F

† Canones Concil. Triden. sess. xiv. cap. 6, p. 77.

that takest away the sins of the world, grant us thy peace!" Thus by assuming the essential prerogatives of God, does "he sit in the temple of God, showing himself that he is God."

5. But this is not all. He actually assumes the *titles* of God. He has allowed himself again and again to be addressed, without rebuke, by the names of the Most High. "We rejoice," says Angelo Politian to Pope Alexander VI. on his election, "to see you raised above all human things, and exalted even to Divinity itself."* On the triumphal arch erected to greet his entry into Rome, the following was inscribed: "Rome was great under Cæsar, now its greatness has risen to the highest pitch under Alexander; and no wonder: the former was a man, the latter a God."† In the dedication of a work to Leo X., published in 1514, Aurelius Serenus speaks of it as a notable event, that an Indian elephant, meeting that pontiff in the street, had "*felt and*

* Bruce's Free Thoughts, p. 32.
† Roscoe's Leo X., vol. ii.

suppliantly adored his divinity!"* "Take care," said Marcellus in the Great Lateran Council to Julius II., speaking in name of the assembled fathers, "take care that we lose not that salvation, that life and health which thou hast given us, for thou art shepherd, thou art physician, thou art governor, thou art husbandman, thou finally art another God upon earth."† Now if there were nothing to condemn the Pope but this, that he has *allowed* such blasphemous names to be bestowed upon him, this of itself would stamp him with guilt of the deepest dye. It was for permitting the multitude to bestow similar appellations upon him, for allowing them to say, "It is the voice of a god, and not of a man," that Herod was smitten of the angel and eaten up of worms. But in point of fact, the Popes themselves have *challenged* such titles as their due. At an early period, Gregory II., writing to the Greek emperor, maintained that "all the churches of the west held Peter as God

* Roscoe's Leo X., vol. ii.
† Labb. tom. xiv. p. 109.

upon earth.* "It is evident," said Pope Nicholas I., "that the pontiff, whom it is certain that pious prince Constantine called God, cannot be at all bound or loosed by the secular power; and it is manifest that God cannot be judged by men."† Pope Martin V. in his instructions to his nuncio at Constantinople, commanded himself to be announced under the following lofty title: "The Most Holy and Most Blessed, possessor of the Heavenly empire, who is Lord on earth, and successor of St Peter, the Christ or Anointed of the Lord, the Lord of the Universe, the Father of kings, the Light of the World, the Sovereign Pontiff, Pope Martin."‡ "Christ," says Boniface VIII. "took Peter into the PARTNERSHIP OF THE UNDIVIDED TRINITY."§ In the gloss on the canon law, approved and passed by Gregory XIII., the Pope is expressly styled "the Lord our God;"‖ and in the de-

* Labb., tom. vii., p. 22.
† Decret. Par. Distinct. 96, cap. 7.
‡ Acta Concil. Senen., Paris, 1612.
§ Sext. Decret. lib. i. tit. 6.
‖ Bull. Gregor. XIII., Rom. 1, Jul. 1580.

cretal issued by *authority* of John XXII., the following occurs: "To believe that our Lord God the Pope might not decree, as he hath decreed, it were a matter of heresy."* Surely he that thus speaks must be the Antichrist, must be the little horn that was "to speak marvellous things against the God of gods." Our ears are shocked by such words; but so familiar are the Pope's immediate subjects with them, that, according to Dr Keith, his common style in Italy, at this hour, is—"Our Lord God the Pope"!!!

6. Such are some of the blasphemies of the Papacy. But this does not exhaust what is contained in the passage of the prophecy under consideration. To complete the picture it is necessary that we contemplate the ADORATION of his holiness. Let any man, nay even an infidel, enter the church of St Peter's at Rome, on the enthronement of a new Pope, and compare what he sees there with this prophecy, and then try if it be possible to resist the conviction, both

* Extrav. Johan. xxii.

that the Pope is the Man of Sin, and that the book which contains such a prediction must be indeed divine. The cardinals have met in secret conclave; for days bribery and corruption have been rife; every artifice has been put in practice by the partizans of the different candidates; but at last the suffrages have been taken, the scrutiny has been made, the election is declared, and *Te Deum* has been sung. His holiness now appears in pomp in St Peter's. Let the reader imagine himself present on such an occasion. Behold the newly elected Pope, seated in state on the high altar, glittering with jewels, and resplendent with scarlet and gold. On that altar lies the wafer god—on that altar stands the crucifix, which all Roman Catholics "worship." *Above* both, is this king of pride "exalted." It is not enough that he *actually* resists the truth and cause of God; but here is he openly exhibited to the world as "exalted above all," that on *earth*, even by Papists themselves, "is *called* God and is worshipped." Clouds of incense ascend before him, and adorations are paid him by the assembled multitude. The cardinals take the lead in the idolatrous rites. "*Venite' adoremus*," ("Come, let us worship him,") they blasphemously exclaim in the words of the 95th Psalm; and all knees are bent in humble adoration. "How often," says Professor Gaussen of Geneva, describing such a scene which he himself had witnessed, "how often, as I viewed him in the midst of his pomp, have I heard this oracle of the Holy Ghost resound within my inmost soul, 'He shall sit as God in the temple of God, showing himself that he is God.'"*

* Gaussen's Geneva and Rome, p. 14.

CHAPTER IV.

The Mystery of Iniquity.

2 THESSALONIANS ii. 5–7.

"Remember ye not, that, when I was yet with you, I told you these things? And now ye know what withholdeth, that he might be revealed in his time. For the MYSTERY OF INIQUITY doth already work: only he who now letteth will let, until he be taken out of the way."

THE apostacy, and the Man of Sin, who was to organise and preside over that apostacy, were not now for the first time brought before the minds of the Christians at Thessalonica. Paul had, ere now, in his preaching, distinctly informed them of the blight that was to come over the Christian church. "Remember ye not," says he, "that when I was yet with you, I told you of these things?" He counted it not enough, as the phrase goes, "to preach the Gospel" to them. He declared to them the whole counsel of God. He put them on their guard against the heresies that were to spring up in the church; and, for this purpose, gave them an outline of its future history. In every healthy period of the church, prophecy has always occupied an important place in the attention of God's faithful ministers. If Paul told the Thessalonians of these things, so many hundred years before the Man of sin was to be revealed, how much more necessary, now that he *is revealed*, that the attention of Christians should be called to them. Yet for a long period, till recently, the prophetic Scriptures, and especially those referring to the apostacy, had fallen into neglect. It had even passed into a maxim, that "the study of unfulfilled prophecy either finds a man mad or makes him so." How derogatory to the Word of God, in which these prophecies are recorded! How utterly opposed to the express declarations of the Scriptures themselves! "Blessed," saith the Spirit of God, at the beginning of the book of Revelation, "blessed is he that readeth, and they that hear the words of this prophecy, and keep those things that are written therein: for the time is at hand." In every prophecy, however much it may stretch into futurity, there is always something that has a bearing upon the present spiritual welfare of the church. Had the believers at Thessalonica only remembered what Paul had told them in his preaching, about the revelation of the Man of sin, they would have been more fortified against the seductions of false teachers, they would not have been needlessly excited and disturbed about the immediate coming of the Lord to judgment. And had professing Christians of the present day been better acquainted with the prophetic descriptions of the character and doom of apostate Rome, there would not have been half the danger that there now is, of seeing it regain its ascendancy over the nations that threw off its yoke at the Reformation. "The sure word of prophecy" is especially intended to shine amid the darkness which God foresaw would come in the latter days upon the world. In it, as in a chart, are accurately laid down all the rocks and quicksands, through the midst of which God's people have to steer their course. By taking heed to its predictions, by comparing them with the aspect of the times, they are not only preserved from the spiritual dangers which prove fatal to others, but their faith is even strengthened by witnessing the spread of *predicted* antichristian error. Thus, while the ungodly around them are walking in darkness, prophecy is not only a light unto their feet and a lamp unto their path; but a growing light—a light, as Goldsmith says of Hope,

> "Which, still as darker grows the night,
> Emits the brighter ray."

At the time that Paul wrote, the seeds were already sown, and germinating, that were afterwards to produce such an abundant harvest of corruption. "*The mystery of iniquity doth already work.*" To the same effect is the testimony of John, "Ye have heard that antichrist shall come; and *even now there are many anti-*

christs." So early did the devil sow his tares; so early did self-righteousness, worldliness, and ambition begin to show themselves; so early did men, like Diotrephes, love to have the pre-eminence in the Christian church. But there was an obstacle to the full development of the mystery of iniquity, and the revelation of antichrist, as the church and the world then stood. What that obstacle was, the apostle had informed the Thessalonians when he had spoken to them on the subject, by word of mouth. At present he thinks not fit to enter on it more particularly than by referring them to his former instructions about it. "*And now ye know what withholdeth, that he might be revealed in his time.*" Now that we know *who is* the Man of Sin, where he is to be found, and what was to be the grand object of his ambition, we need be at no loss, as to the obstacle that hindered his full development, and withheld him from rising to the summit of his power. It was to be in Rome, on the throne of the Cæsars, that the Man of sin was to sit, and as Head of the Church, to lord it over the prostrate nations of Europe. But when the apostle wrote, Cæsar occupied the throne himself; and so long as the imperial power continued to flourish, the selfish designs of ambitious and worldly churchmen were kept within bounds. For centuries, even amid persecution, the assumptions of the Roman bishops were steadily rising; but it was not till after the irruption of the Goths, the dismemberment of the Roman empire, and the evacuation of Rome itself by the representatives of the imperial power, that the Man of sin began to stand forth before the world, in his decidedly antichristian character. It was to the imperial power, then, beyond doubt, that Paul here referred, as withholding the revelation of the Man of Sin, and as destined to do so, "until it should be taken out of the way." There were obvious reasons why the Spirit of God did not speak more explicitly on this subject, lest the pagan emperors, sufficiently disposed to persecute Christianity at any rate, should be provoked by a prediction of the downfall of their empire, to ravage the Christian church without mercy. But there was enough revealed, though under mystical symbols, in other parts of the word of God, in Daniel especially, and the book of Revelation, to lead the people of God to form right conclusions on this subject. And it is interesting to know, that the most distinguished writers among the early Christians, whom the Papists themselves pretend to regard as authorities, took the very same view on this point, *before* the Man of Sin was revealed, that Protestant commentators have almost universally done *since* his revelation. "As long as the empire shall be able to make itself feared," saith Chrysostom, "no man shall readily submit himself to antichrist; but after the empire shall be dissolved, antichrist shall invade the vacant throne of the empire, and shall labour to concentrate in himself the power both of God and of man."* Precisely similar are the statements of Tertullian, Ambrose, and Augustine, all of whom used to pray for the continuance of the Roman empire in its strength, that the reign of

* Chrysost. Opera, Tom. xi. p. 530. Paris, 1734.

antichrist might be retarded. When, therefore, the Popish translators of the Rhemish Testament, in a strain of affected humility, boast that "Jesus hath now made all the Roman emperors, and princes of the world, to know him, and hath given the seat of the Cæsars to his poor servants, Peter and his successors,"* they thereby bear their testimony, according to the view of these fathers, to the fact, that "he that letted, no longer lets, but has now been taken out of the way;" that the "mystery of iniquity" has had ample room to perfect itself; and that the "Man of sin" must long ago have been "revealed."

In the Church of Rome, beyond question, the "mystery of iniquity" is to be found; and how wonderfully descriptive of Popery, and its mode of working, is the name by which the Spirit of God hath here characterised it. Popery is one grand system of consecrated wickedness. Under a semblance of holiness, and humility, and charity, and self-denial, a structure of priestcraft, and crime, and superstition has been reared,

* Rhemish Testament. Note on Acts xxv. 19.

which is unparalleled in the history of the world. While accommodating itself to the corruption of human nature, it makes use of the leading truths of the Gospel only to gild the rottenness of its own moral pollution. It works the will of Satan in the name of Him who came into the world to destroy the works of the devil. Under fair shows and plausible professions, it knows how to introduce the most pestilential errors; and it is this that makes it so dangerous to men, who have only a superficial knowledge of the truth, who have only a form of godliness, but are destitute of the power of it. It artfully makes the very fragments of truth which such men have floating in their minds, the means of blinding and misleading them. This might be illustrated in innumerable ways; but a few instances may suffice.

1. The doctrine of the *Church*, its unity, and its privileges, is cunningly perverted by the Man of Sin for his own purposes. The Church unquestionably occupies a very important position in the word of God. Christ loved it, loved it

only, and gave his life for it. It is his bride, it is his body; and every member of it is dear to him as the apple of his eye. Glorious things are spoken of the Church, the city of the living God; but it is to the spiritual church, the church composed of renewed and sanctified souls, of men united by faith to the living Head, that all these things are appropriated. The church visible, and the church spiritual, are entirely distinct. Many are admitted into the former, who have neither part nor lot in the latter. Now Popery confounds the distinctions between these two, and mere professors are willing enough to have it so. Those things which are true alone of the spiritual church, it applies indiscriminately to the members of the outward church. It is quite true, when properly understood, that the people of God's holy Church are "*all* righteous," and shall certainly be saved; and that none else shall be so. Rome leads her devotees to believe, that all within the outward pale of the church, who submit to her authority, are without doubt God's true and holy people;

and that, consequently, their immortal interests are safe. Thus, by the *name* of the Church the people are deluded; and the power of the priesthood is maintained. The people are lulled into a false and fatal security, while the clergy are made the arbiters of their everlasting destiny. For to the latter it belongs to admit them to the privileges of the Church, or to exclude them from its communion; and on them, therefore, it depends, whether a man's soul shall be lost or saved. Thus, through the perversion of an important truth, are the foundations laid for spiritual despotism.

2. The very abasement of a sinner, conscious of guilt and unworthiness, in the hands of Antichrist, is made a stepping-stone to the introduction of idolatry. Humility is certainly a Christian grace, and a Christian can never feel sufficiently humble. In the worship of God especially, it becomes him deeply to feel his own unworthiness; and to have a sense of his sinfulness imprinted on his inmost soul. Can such a one as he, then, so unholy, so unworthy, dare to

lift his eyes directly to Christ, the Holy One and the Just, who is so infinitely exalted. No; surely it were better to apply to some one of the glorified saints or angels, in the presence of God, who, as creatures, are not so immensely above him, who will present his supplications to God's Son, and thus gain for him an attention and acceptance, which he could not expect for himself. Thus does Popery deceive those who listen to its serpent tongue. The pretence looks fair; but it is a mystery of iniquity. What saith the word of God? It characterises this worshipping of saints or angels, as a "voluntary humility," a humility which God does not require, which he does not approve, which he utterly condemns—a humility which will "beguile" those who practise it, of the "reward" which is promised to the true believer. The language of Christ to all, to the very chief of sinners, is not, "Go to this saint—apply to that angel," but—"Come unto ME." And when HE gives so kind, so free, so gracious, so universal an invitation, to doubt his willingness to receive the most unworthy, and to have recourse to other intercessors, is a reflection on his sincerity, a disparagement of his mercy and goodness. It supposes that there may be more love, more condescension, more compassion in a creature than in Him, who, though in the form of God, and thinking it not robbery to be equal with God, *humbled* himself, and became obedient unto death, even the death of the cross, that sinners, that rebels, might be saved. Instead, therefore, of manifesting humility, such supplications betoken the highest presumption, and spring from the father of lies. And the result of such "voluntary humility" has been worthy of its origin. It has flooded the Church that encouraged it with the rankest idolatry. It has utterly led away the laity of the Church of Rome from the worship of the one living and true God, to the worship of those who by nature are no gods. "I am sure I do not exaggerate," says the author of "Rome in the Nineteenth Century," when I say that throughout Italy, Spain, Portugal, and every country, where the Roman Catholic is the exclusive religion of the people, for one knee bent to God, thousands are bowed before the shrine of the Virgin and the saints." Thus, has this "voluntary humility" debased the minds of the people, thus has it paved the way for the enthronement of the Virgin above the true God, and the exaltation of the Pope "above all that is called God and is worshipped."

3. The pious feelings of devout but half-enlightened minds have, in like manner, been abused to the corruption of Christianity. When the priests first began to depreciate preaching, and to cry up the superior importance of making the house of God more and more a "house of prayer," how few were there who could have imagined what such fair professions would end in! It looked so much like piety, it had so much the air of godliness, to labour to promote devotional feeling among the people, that it would have seemed almost uncharitable to hint, nay even to suspect, that any snake lurked in the grass. Yet here was the mystery of iniquity at work. So long as

the word of God was duly read, and expounded in the pulpit, the enlightenment thus diffused was unfavourable to the ambitious aims of the clergy, and retarded the spiritual despotism they wished to erect. Hence the zeal among many for public prayers; hence the cry for additional devotional services; that preaching might first be thrust into a corner, and then gradually abandoned.* The object was at last gained. Then were all the arts of the Man of Sin called into requisition to perpetuate his power, and to keep the people in contented ignorance. And to an astonishing degree has he succeeded. Rome has engrafted on the worship of God all the attractions of the theatre. She has contrived a gorgeous and splendid ceremonial, which, while it gratifies the taste, and fascinates the senses, soothes the conscience, lulls asleep in sin, and flatters with the hopes of heaven, those who live in the gall of bitterness and bond of iniqui-

* Puseyism in this, as in many other respects, shows a striking family likeness to Rome. The Tracts for the Times call preaching "an instrument, which Scripture has never much recommended."

ty. While the natural feelings are moved, the imagination pleased, and the mind excited, men, who have not one particle of spiritual feeling or true devotion, are rapt up to the third heavens in their own conceit, and led to fancy themselves uncommonly devout. Thus does Babylon "intoxicate the nations with the wine of her fornication." The ingredients in her wine-cup are skilfully mingled; and music, sculpture, painting and architecture, all exquisite in their kind, form the intoxicating draught, which the Grand Sorceress puts into the hands of her votaries. Every thing in her worship is formed for effect; every thing tends to keep her worshippers in blind and willing subjection. All that is imposing in spectacle, and enchanting in melody, is combined in the services of Rome. The very spirit of the world is enshrined in the Holy of holies; and while the lusts of the eyes, and the pride of life are pampered and gratified, the poor deluded Papists believe themselves ripening for heaven. To those who wish to serve God and the world at the same time, there is no religion so easy, so palatable, so pleasing, as the religion of Antichrist.

4. How fair, how plausible at first sight might have seemed the pretexts for clerical celibacy. "He that is unmarried careth for the things of the Lord, that he may be holy both in body and in spirit, that he may please the Lord." So saith an apostle. What then should hinder any one to bind himself with a vow so to continue? What should hinder the clergy, above all, who ought to be specially devoted to the Lord, from being "forbidden to marry?" Much. "All cannot receive this saying," said he, who knew what is in man, "but those to whom it is given." It was self-righteousness that first introduced the perpetual celibacy of the clergy; the self-interest of the Papacy established it; and its results have been most deplorable. "It seems fair," says Bishop Jewell, "and a matter of great holiness. But there is a mystery in it; the mystery of iniquity. It is a gulf, it is a sea, it is a world, it is a hell,

of iniquity, and the vilest villany that ever crept into the church of God."* This is strong language, but not stronger than the nature of the case amply warrants. It was no love for holiness, no real desire for the spiritual welfare of men; but a base and wicked design to bind the world in abject slavery to the see of Rome, that induced Pope after Pope to labour so earnestly for the enforcement of clerical celibacy, until Hildebrand ultimately carried his point. While the clergy were allowed to marry, they had other interests than those of the papacy: their affection for their families divided their allegiance with Rome, and identified them more with the people, than was expedient for the grasping ambition of the mitred king. To cut them off from all the endearments of social life, to isolate them entirely from the people, was perceived to be the only way to bind them indissolubly to the chair of St Peter, to infuse the true *esprit du corps* into the whole body of the clergy, and to make the aggrandizement and

* British Reformers, Jewell, p. 228.

glory of the church the grand aim and object of their lives. This, and this only, was what Hildebrand cared for; and so the Papacy might be glorified, it mattered not to him, that God's ordinance was outraged, that affectionate hearts were broken, that the dearest ties were rent asunder, that the sluices were set wide open for deluging Europe with a flood of debauchery.

Some indeed in the present day have attempted to whitewash this policy of Gregory VII., and no less a champion than M. Guizot has appeared in his behalf. According to him, Hildebrand was actuated by the most praiseworthy designs, and a real regard for the welfare of society. "We have been accustomed," says he, "to consider Gregory VII. as a man who wished to render every thing immutable; as an enemy to intellectual development; to social progress; as a man whose desire was to to retain the world in a stationary or retrograde condition. Nothing is farther from the truth. Gregory VII. was a despotic *reformer*, like Charlemagne and Peter the Great. He effected nearly as much for the ecclesiastical order, as Charlemagne in France, and Peter the Great in Russia, accomplished for civil existence. His aim was to reform the church, and through the church to reform civil society; to introduce into the world a greater degree of morality, justice, and order."* Such is M. Guizot's opinion of the character and policy of Gregory VII. M. Guizot professes to be a Protestant. Had he read a book with which Protestants ought to be familiar, he would have seen that those who "forbid to marry," are characterized as "speaking lies in hypocrisy, having their consciences seared with a hot iron." If ecclesiastical history says true, Gregory VII. was no exception to this statement. But how can any man of common sense speak of the *absolute* prohibition of marriage to the clergy as a "reform," as a means of improving the church, and through the church, of promoting the welfare of society? How could it possibly tend "to introduce into the world a greater degree of morality, justice, and order,"

* Lectures on Civilisation, Lect. vi.

to make marriage, which is "honourable in all men," a sin of at *least* equal guilt with fornication or adultery? This of itself necessarily tended to obliterate the distinctions between right and wrong; to pervert the dictates of conscience, to introduce a factitious morality, and to sap the very foundations of society. And who does not see that when a thing, in itself innocent, is arbitrarily classed with heinous crimes, the guilt and turpitude of these crimes is necessarily brought down? Conscience, in spite of man's prohibitions, can never look upon marriage in any man as a very *serious* fault. When, therefore, marriage and adultery are placed on the same level, the natural depravity of man easily leads him to think of the latter with but little abhorrence. What then could be expected from men unalterably devoted to a state of life for which nature did not fit them, from men exposed to continual temptation, and with such perverted ideas of religion, but that which has actually ensued? It would have been a miracle had it been otherwise. The celibacy of the clergy has made the "Holy Apostolic Church" of Rome, literally as well as spiritually, the "Mother of Abominations." Popes and cardinals, priests and prelates, are shown by the authentic records of history to have wallowed in the most gross and brutal licentiousness. At the Reformation, both in Scotland and England, the monasteries, in many instances, were proved before Parliamentary commissioners to be no better than so many brothels, and scenes for the perpetration of such wickedness, as brought down fire and brimstone from heaven on Sodom and Gomorrah. The secular clergy vied with the monks in profligacy. If any one should suspect that these statements are coloured by party feeling as coming from Protestants, then we appeal to Roman Catholics themselves. What was the argument employed by the Roman senate to dissuade the Pope, when meditating the suppression of the licensed brothels at Rome, from carrying his design into effect? Thuanus, the Roman Catholic historian, informs us that they petitioned for their continuance, on the ground that thus *the clergy might be prevented from violating their wives and daughters.** The testimony of certain Roman Catholic divines of Germany, who presented a remonstrance against the enforcement of celibacy to the Pope in 1564, accompanied by a letter from the Emperor is to the very same effect. "Among fifty Catholic priests," say they, "hardly one will be found who is not a notorious fornicator;" and they considered it "a great absurdity not to admit married clerks, and to tolerate fornicators."† Would these men calumniate their order? Would they calumniate them to the Pope? Assuredly not. The profligacy of the clergy had become notorious, and at the time of the Reformation, all Germany, Popish as well as Protestant, cried out against it. In the diet of Nuremberg, which sat in 1522, a remonstrance was drawn up in name of the cities, states, and princes who composed it, entitled "*Centum Gravamina*,"‡ in which the corrup-

* Thuan. Histor. Lib. xxxix. p. 779. Frankfort, 1625.

† Soave Polano, lib. viii. p. 805. A Lond., 1609.

‡ The Hundred Grievances.

tions of the church were loudly complained of, and redress urgently demanded from the Pope. What a picture of the moral state of the clergy do we find in the following passages of that celebrated document :—"The officials," says the diet, uttering the unanimous voice of all Germany, "the officials, possessed of a detestable avarice, not only do not prohibit usury, but permit and uphold it. Nay, for an annual tribute levied on monks and priests, they permit them publicly to keep concubines and harlots, by whom they have children. . . . Most of the bishops not only allow the clergy to keep concubines, on paying a tax for them; but even if there are some honest and well-principled priests who wish to live virtuously, they too are compelled to pay, under pretext that the bishop has need of money. After that, they may either live chastely, or keep concubines, as they may have a mind." (Articles 75 and 91.) "The only good thing that remained," says Jurieu, commenting on this passage, "was, that they were not *compelled* to keep a concubine." But to what a state of degradation and moral pollution must the clergy have sunk, when the states of Germany felt constrained thus to expose their turpitude!* And what led to all this? The pretence to "angelic sanctity," on the part of those who forbade to marry. Verily it is a mystery of iniquity.

5. The practice of auricular confession, that fountain of wickedness, that grand pillar of spiritual despotism, grew up also from apparently the most natural and harmless beginnings. Men deeply concerned about their salvation will often feel themselves in doubt and darkness as to their state. To whom could they more natur-

* Jurieu, Histoire du Calvin. et du Pap. tom. i. Rotterdam 1683. The evidence of the unbounded licentiousness of the priests of Rome, from Roman Catholic sources, would fill a volume. Some of them have even gloried in their shame. "Friends," said Cardinal Hugo, addressing the citizens of Lyons, at the breaking up of the general council held in that city, "we have effected a work of great utility and charity here. When we came to Lyons we found three or four brothels in it, and we have left at our departure, only one. But this extends, without interruption, from the eastern to the western gate of the city." Matthew Paris, 794.

ally look for help in their spiritual perplexities than to their pastors, to those who are over them in the Lord, and who watch for their souls as those that must give account? In an earnest period of the church there will always be many such, seeking guidance and direction. But how can spiritual counsel be appropriate, unless the person seeking it unbosom himself to his counsellor? There is an obvious necessity in the nature of the case for some measure of confidential communication. If pure religion prevail among the people, if zeal for the salvation of souls supremely inspire the clergy, such spiritual communing between pastor and people will be not only harmless, but blessed. The people will seek only instruction from the minister; the minister will desire nothing more than to be the helper of his people's joy. But if superstition be spreading, if the clergy be more anxious to bind the people to themselves than to lead them to Christ, such intercourse will assuredly end in mischief. And in the Church of Rome it did so. A corrupt and ambitious priesthood saw the advantage it gave them to have the people unfolding to them the secret thoughts of their hearts. By little and little, the importance of such confessions was magnified. The practice grew into a positive duty, and at last it was enjoined as indispensable to salvation. The clergy were no longer the helpers of their people's faith, but arbiters of their state, empowered authoritatively to adjudge them to happiness or woe. For the due discharge of their functions, to enable them to pronounce absolution on just and proper grounds, the most searching examination of course was necessary.* Now the mischief of this is obvious and manifold.

It is of the most degrading and corrupting tendency on those who are subjected to it, and fitted to obliterate from their minds every trace of virtuous feeling that has survived the ruins of the fall. Through means of the questions of the Confessional, ingenuous youth become acquainted, and are rendered familiar with, vices of the most abominable kind, which they could

* See Note G.

never otherwise have heard of. From this polluting influence in the Church of Rome there is no escape. Nay, if a young female, under such a scrutiny, show symptoms of embarrassment or modesty, the confessor is required to take pains that her "bashfulness and modesty be overcome." Is this an injunction of the dark ages? Is this a practice recommended only in Italy or Spain? No. It is in force at this day, at our own doors, in the popish parishes of Ireland. The injunction I have quoted is taken from Bailly, one of the text-books of Maynooth. And if, after all efforts on the part of the confessor, the fair penitent still cannot be prevailed on to give a distinct answer to the most abominable questions, she is pronounced "unworthy of absolution," that is, she is left in a state exposing her to the *pains of hell!* What church but that of Antichrist could make the modesty of a virtuous mind—that fence which God himself has set around morality—a crime deserving of damnation!

While the Confessional is thus polluting to

those who are subjected to its interrogatories, it is not less so to the priests who put them. What has been already said may sufficiently prove this; but there are yet "greater abominations than these." Will it be believed that the unmarried Roman Catholic priests of Ireland are instructed in their class-books to interrogate married women as to the whole intercourse that takes place between them and their husbands? Yet such is the fact, as any one may see by reference to the fourth volume of Bailly's Moral Theology, p. 483, or the instructions in regard to the Confessional contained in the sixth volume of Dens.* What but the most depraved and brutalized imagination could have dictated such a sytem? What but contamination can be the result to those who have the working of it? "When the priest," says the Rev. James Godkin, himself formerly a Roman Catholic, "commences his duties, a new scene opens. He is excited by the novelty, the piquant curiosity, and the powerful interest that encircles the Confessional. The

* Dens' Theology, pp. 124, 285, 286.

secrets which are there in loneliness and silence whispered into his ear become the subject of his daily lucubrations, and his nocturnal visions. There is incessantly passing through his mind a stream of impurity, which is retained fetid and foul in the reservoir of memory, alas! too tenacious of evil."*

With such influences for evil continually operating, with such facilities for poisoning the moral principle of women ever at command, could any one, even apart from all experience, ever imagine that *unmarried* priests could generally come unscathed from the ordeal to which they are exposed? If he did, the history of all Roman Catholic countries ought to convince him to the contrary. Auricular confession and clerical celibacy together have demoralized every country wherever they have prevailed. "A large amount," says an able writer, "of seduction, fornication, and adultery, has come from the Confessional. By means of going to the priest in private to confess their sins, many

* Guide from the Church of Rome to the Church of Christ.

females have been led to vice and unchastity, and been utterly undone. Instead of being improved from sinful to holy, they have been made immoral, abandoned, lewd, and lost. Their confessor has been their corrupter, and instead of taking away their sins, has robbed them of their virtue, cheated them of their chastity, and made them twofold more children of hell than they were before. I quote the following from Howitt's History of Priestcraft, chapter xiv.—'Father Anthony Joseph has for eight years past been continually plunged in the abominable practice of sinning with women at the time they come to confess, and even in the place where he confessed them, after which he gave them absolution, and administered the sacrament to them! He told them that these actions need not give them any concern, since all their fathers, the bishops, and the Pope himself, observed the same practice.'"* Knowing the general licentiousness of the clergy, knowing the

* Rogers' Antipopery. Michelet, in his "Priests, Women, and Families," shows the deplorable working of the confessional in France at this day. See Note H.

power of seduction which the confessional puts into their hands, do we need to wonder that the senate of Rome petitioned for the continuance of the licensed brothels, that thus, perchance, the purity of their homes, and the comfort of their firesides, might be safe from violation? But what a wretched, what a deplorable, what an accursed system, to bear the abused name of Christ! Who would not cry, with a full heart, How long, O Lord, holy and true, dost thou not judge them that corrupt the earth? Who would not pray for the day when Babylon the Great shall be brought low,—when it shall be cast like a millstone into the sea, and shall rise no more at all?

Such is the effect of auricular confession upon *morals.* But in the hands of wicked priests, all bound by the strongest ties to the Papacy, what an engine for ecclesiastical tyranny! The "little horn" of Daniel, which every Protestant commentator of note agrees in identifying with the Man of sin, is represented as "having eyes like the eyes of a man." In the Confessional, we see the astonishing significancy of the prophetic emblem. From the seven hills of the "eternal city," the Pope sees all, and knows all, that goes on throughout the earth. Every priest is one of his spies, whose grand business it is to watch, to search out, and report to head-quarters, every thing that affects the interests of the Papacy, every thing that may either damage its cause, or promote its aggrandisement. By means of the revelations of the Confessional, the secrets, the tempers, the weaknesses, the wickedness, of all the Roman Catholic courts of Europe, are accurately known at Rome. Nay, the see of St Peter's is better informed of the feelings and designs of professedly Protestant sovereigns than many who are nearer home. For where is there a Protestant court at this day, in which there is not some one or other of the confidential servants, who is an adherent of the Man of sin? From these the confessor, in the discharge of his recognised duty, can extract all that it concerns his church to know; and thus Protestant or Roman Catholic princes shall not utter a whisper in their bed-chamber, but the echo of it shall be heard at Rome. By means of auricular confession, the Pope is in reality the universal *Overseer* of Christendom. By its means "coming events cast their shadows before" in the Vatican, long before they elsewhere appear above the horizon. By its means he knows how to set one sovereign against another, so as to break the power of those who oppose him; by it, he knows when to speak, and when to be silent; when it will most further his ends to promote rebellion in Ireland, and when, as he did about a year ago, to issue his mandate to his vassals in that country "to obey the powers that be." In every respect, then, the Confessional is the most cunningly devised instrument that hell itself could invent, at once for debauching the minds both of clergy and people, and binding them all in the most abject bondage to the throne of Antichrist.

6. Prayer for the dead, that fertile source of superstition among the people, and of wealth to the priests, is maintained by plausible ap-

peals to the most kindly and benevolent feelings of our nature. If you hear, say the priests, that a friend is just dead, of whose fitness for heaven you have anxious fears, what is the first prompting of your heart with regard to him? Is it not to wish that his soul may be safe? and if to wish, why not to pray? May not this instinctive feeling of nature be the voice of God within you, calling you to supplication in his behalf? And can it be right, nay, is it not cruel, to check the feelings of humanity, in regard to one who is dear to you, but of whose preparation for blessedness you have no assurance? Supposing prayer should do no good, what harm could it do? Thus does popery insinuate itself in angel guise; and thus are unstable souls beguiled into the meshes of Romanism at this day. The proposition in this form seems not so very formidable; but once give way in this matter to the blind impulse of feeling, and you have commenced your descent on that inclined plane which will speedily land you in all the absurdities of purgatory. The whole tenor of God's

Word implies, that at *death* men enter on an unchangeable state, that "he who is holy then is holy still, and that he who is filthy then is filthy still," and that for ever. To suppose that those who depart this life unfit for heaven, can ever be *rendered* fit, is subversive of the whole Gospel. If we can only believe that sinners dying in unpardoned sin, can any how get sin pardoned after death, it is easy to take the next step, and to believe that pardon comes, after passing through penal suffering or purgatorial fire. Grant the existence of purgatory, and the efficacy of prayers for the dead, and you have granted to the priests all that they need for drawing to themselves the wealth of the world. What would a rich man with a burdened conscience, on his dying bed, not give, if he was persuaded that, by leaving that money, which he can no longer keep, for prayers and masses for his soul, he should save himself from torment, or mitigate and shorten his anguish after death? What sacrifices would affectionate relatives not make, for the repose of their departed friends, if they really believed that priestly prayers and masses would deliver them from misery? This doctrine of purgatory is the very climax, the copestone of the grand fabric of the mystery of iniquity. While it flourished, wealth unbounded flowed into the coffers of Rome. In one church of that city, the church of St Paul's, such was the concourse of strangers, during the dark ages, that according to Gibbon,* two priests stood night and day, with rakes in their hands, to collect without counting, the heaps of gold that were poured on the altar. Goods, and money, and houses, and lands, were bequeathed to the church for this purpose; and had not the statute of Mortmain interfered, the whole property of England would have been swallowed up by the rapacious clergy. It is one of the ominous signs of the present day, that that statute which even Popish monarchs found it absolutely necessary for the safety of the state to enact, in order that bounds might be set to the rapacity of the church, is now being relaxed

* Gibbon's Decline and Fall, vol. xii. p. 311.

or repealed by Protestant legislators, and that for the express purpose of allowing facilities for the aggrandizement of the Church of Rome. How true is the maxim of Coleridge, that "experience is like a lantern on the stern, that shines only on the waves behind us!" If it was only of their wealth that men were cheated by this figment of purgatory, the evil were comparatively slight. But the ruin which it works to men's souls is infinitely more momentous. It checks repentance, it emboldens men in sin, it encourages them to lead an ungodly life, in the vain hope of atoning for it after death. No wonder, then, that all popish countries are overrun with immorality.

But from how apparently small a seed, in this, as in the other cases already specified, did so great a harvest of evil spring. It was this that made the mystery of iniquity so successful in deceiving the world. Had the hideous system appeared at once in all its deformity, "full formed, with warning rattle, and hissing tongue," men would have been on their guard, they would have been frightened, they would have been roused to exertion to check its progress. But coming as it did with so much that was plausible, with so little to alarm any but those who were spiritually enlightened, few gave themselves any concern as to its progress, and it was allowed to take its course. Thus the Alpine snowball, which rolls down the mountain's side, is at first trifling, and fitted to inspire but little alarm; but, as it passes from steep to steep, accumulating as it goes, it appals the spectator, mocks opposition, and at last overwhelms in ruin towns and villages.*

Popery has not forgot the way in which it gained its early triumphs. It still works with "all deceivableness of unrighteousness." Whenever it is necessary, it can disguise, it can suppress, it can soften down, its revolting principles. It can suit itself to all times and circumstances. Without abandoning one of its essential doctrines, it can profess liberality with liberals, and shout for reform with reformers. While

* See Edgar's Variations.

stigmatizing the principle of private judgment as one of the "rude errors of the reformation," it can talk of the rights of conscience, and gain credit as an advocate of civil and religious liberty.* While acting on the maxim that ignorance is the mother of devotion, it can manage to get itself extolled as the ardent friend of universal education. All that is "lovely, and fair, and of good report," it will counterfeit, that it may deceive the nations, that it may bring them to worship at its shrine; that it may have the power to trample all knowledge, all virtue, all freedom in the dust. One reason that so many in the present day allow themselves to be imposed upon by it, is, because they have forgotten the name by which the Spirit of God has described it. They forget, that it is "The mystery of iniquity." Without keeping this grand truth constantly before us, we shall never be able to understand its plans, its policy, its professions. With this clue in our hand, we may be guided safely through many a labyrinth.

* See Letter of O'Connell to Editor of Christian Instructor, Nov. 1835.

CHAPTER V.

The Lawless One.

2 THESSALONIANS ii. 8.

And then shall that WICKED be revealed, whom the Lord shall consume with the spirit of his mouth, and destroy with the brightness of his coming.

THE name *Wicked*, by which the Man of Sin is here characterised, properly signifies in the original, the LAWLESS ONE,* and is wonderfully descriptive of the pretensions of the Papacy. The Pope claims an exemption from all law, natural and revealed, human and divine; and in this respect Popery is even worse than heathenism itself. "The Gentiles, who had not" the revealed law

* ὁ ἀνομος.

of God, felt bound by their own consciences, to do much "that was contained in the law." But Popery uproots at once the law of nature, and the law of the Bible, and substitutes the mere will of the Pope in its stead. While every soul is bound to obey the Pope, the Pope is bound by no law, either of God or of man. This the Popes and their parasites have asserted again and again. Pope Innocent III., for instance, declared that "he could dispense above the law of God, and of injustice could make justice."* "If the Pope," said Boniface VIII. "regardless of his own salvation, and of the salvation of his brethren, should be found unprofitable, and carry with him innumerable people in troops to the devil, no mortal is to presume to reprove his faults, for he being to judge all, is to be judged by none."† Cardinal Bellarmine, one of the highest authorities in the Papal Church, does not hesitate to say, "that the Pope doth whatever he listeth, even things unlawful,

* Gr. Decret. ix. c. 3.

† Bon. Mart. ap. Decret. Distinct. 40. cap. 6.

and *is more than God.*" And again, "Though the Pope should err in enjoining vices and prohibiting virtues, yet would the Church be bound to believe the vices to be virtues, if it would avoid sinning against its own conscience."* These are no random or inconsiderate expressions. They are the necessary assertion of the power which the Pope is well known to exercise. It is unquestionable that the Pope has *directly* annulled some of the acknowledged laws of God. He has had the daring presumption to lay his hand on the decalogue, and to erase from it the second commandment. Even in catechisms published within the British Islands, the second commandment is altogether expunged. In Dr James Butler's, for instance, the two first commandments are literally given thus: "*Q.* Say the ten commandments of God? *A.* 1. I am the Lord thy God, thou shalt not have strange gods before me. 2. Thou shalt not take the name of the Lord thy God

* Bellarm. De Pontifice, lib. iv., cap. v., published at Rome by *authority*, in 1842.

in vain."* He has treated the fourth in an equally sacrilegious manner. He has abrogated the holy rest of the Sabbath, and appointed other sacred times of his own. In the catechisms published by authority in Italy, "Remember to keep the feasts," is substituted for the solemn injunction of the Lord, "Remember the Sabbath day to keep it holy," thus identifying himself with the little horn, that "thinks to change *times* and laws."†

In the matter of consanguinity he claims power to forbid what God permits, and to permit what God forbids. "If any one shall say," says the Council of Trent, "that those degrees only of consanguinity and affinity, which are expressed in Scripture, can hinder marriage from being contracted, or render it void when it has been contracted, or that the Church has not the power of dispensing in some of those degrees, and determining that others shall hinder or destroy, let him be ac-

* Butler, p. 37. 1843.

† The Pope's claim to *dispense* with the solemn obligation of an *oath*, we have already seen, Chap. I.

cursed."* Who but the *Lawless One* could assert such a doctrine? And not only does the Man of Sin give his sanction to incestuous marriages to those who can afford to pay for them, but the ground on which such base transactions are defended, stamps him with additional infamy. "A dispensation," says Dens, "is granted for certain reasonable causes which are styled *sine causa* (without cause), namely, when a noble person, or one of honourable family asks a dispensation without stating the particular ground, and then a greater pecuniary tax is imposed, to be converted to pious uses. St Thomas observes, that this implies no respect of persons; because the public safety depends more on the powerful than on the common people; and it specially concerns the Church, to have the more powerful not opposed to her, but favourable and under obligations to her."† It has been often represented as a calumny against the Church of Rome, to say that it maintains the principle that the "end sanctifies the means," but here,

* Sess. xxiv. can. 2.

† Dens., vol. viii. p. 295.

amid much hypocritical casuistry, the doctrine is broadly laid down. The grand end to be aimed at is the interest of "the Church;" the means for the attainment of that end is, the "favour" of the great and the "powerful;" and that favour is to be secured by granting authority, without asking questions, and without the least knowledge of the circumstances, for the contracting of marriages, however impure, however incestuous. It was, doubtless, on this principle that Pope Clement VII. offered Henry VIII. a dispensation to have two wives at the same time. The pretext about "converting the money to pious uses," and the attempt to elude the charge of having "respect to persons,' are too glaring to impose upon any man of common discernment. On the principle here laid down, there is no villany that may not be sanctioned; not one of the eternal laws of God that may not be trampled on.

Now, it is vain to say, that this is a mere private opinion of Dens, and that the Papacy is not answerable for it. The principle here propounded, is not half so *grossly* asserted, as it is by the society of the Jesuits, which, after its suppression in the last century, has in the beginning of this, been solemnly re-established by Papal authority, as *the ablest bulwark of the faith of Rome.* The most distinguished advocates of Jesuitism, as shown by the celebrated Pascal, in their writings, subvert all law, human and Divine. Their whole system is framed for the purpose of exalting the Papacy on the ruins alike of morality and religion. Provided the authority of Rome is submitted to, it is directly taught that the love of God, and the love of man, may equally be dispensed with. Incredible as it might seem, the fact is undeniable.

In proof of the first statement, that the love of God, the sum of the first table of the moral law, is completely set aside, let the reader only peruse the following passages from Pascal: "When, asks Escobar, is a person obliged to cherish a real affection for God? Suarez says, It is sufficient to love him a little previous to the moment of death. Vasquez, that it is enough to love him in the very moment of dying; others, at baptism; some, at the seasons of contrition; others, upon festivals. Hurtado de Mendoza states, that we are under an obligation to love God once in a-year, and that we are kindly treated in not being obliged to do it more frequently. But Father Conink believes, that we are under an obligation to do so once in three or four years; and Filiutius says, it is probable that we are not rigorously obliged to it every five years. When then? This question he refers to a wise man's own judgment."* This of itself is bad enough; but Suarez goes on to argue at great length, that "we are not so much commanded to love God, as not to hate him." Nay, this exemption from loving God, is represented as the great benefit or advantage which Christians have above the Jews, in consequence of the incarnation and death of the Son of God. Well might Pascal indignantly exclaim, "What! will the blood of Jesus Christ procure us an exemption from loving him? Before the incar-

* Les Provinciales, Let. x. pp. 172—3. Paris, 1829.

nation, mankind were obliged to love God; but since God so loved the world, as to give his only begotten Son, shall the world, thus mercifully redeemed by him, be discharged from loving him? Strange divinity of our times! To dare to take off the curse which Paul pronounces against those who love not the Lord Jesus! . . . This is the mystery of iniquity complete! Open your eyes at last, my good father, and if the former errors of your casuists are not discernible enough to strike you, may these last withdraw you by their glaring impieties.*

But the love of man is as thoroughly made void, as the love of God. Hear what the holy fathers say of the feelings which children may entertain towards their parents. "For what concerns love," Dicastillus saith, "that it is not *altogether certain* that a child can lawfully desire the death of his father, or rejoice in it, because of the inheritance that may come to him thereby; but he believes that he *sins not mortally* in rejoicing, not in his death, considered as an

* Les Provinciales, Let. x. p. 176.

evil to his father, but as a lawful means appointed of God, for him to obtain the succession; not because some evil befel the father, but some good to the son."* Tambourin takes up and discusses the same question, and at once boldly determines it in the affirmative. "If you desire," says he, "the death of your father upon some condition, the answer is easy, that *you lawfully may.* For if one should say in himself, if my father should die, I should enjoy his estate, in this case he would not rejoice in his father's death, but in his inheritance."† After this way of treating the first commandment with promise, we need not be surprised that all the other commandments of the second table, are allowed to be unscrupulously trampled on whenever occasion may require. And when such a lawful occasion may occur, no one need be at a loss to determine. "A person," says Basil Pontius, quoted and approved by Father Bauny, in his treatise on penance, "may seek an occasion to sin directly and by itself *primo et per se*,

* Jesuits' Morals, p. 298. † Ibid. p. 299.

when either *our own temporal* or spiritual good, or that of our neighbour demands it."* The insertion of the "*good of our neighbour*," is here of course nothing more than a blind. How do they carry out their doctrine? Listen to the principle which they lay down for the regulation of those to whom is committed the administration of justice. "A judge," say they, "owes *justice* to all, and therefore he cannot *sell* it; but he does not owe *injustice;* and therefore he may sell *that*."† The Jesuits have ever been particularly accommodating to great men, and men in authority; but they set no bounds to the privileges of the clergy. There are no principles of morality which they may not warrantably contemn when the interests of their order are concerned. "Upon what occasions," asks one of their Catechisms, "may a monk quit his habit, without incurring excommunication?" and the answer is given, "Among many

* Les Provinc. Lett. v. p. 66.

† Les Provinciales, Lett. viii. p. 130. These are Pascal's own words, but the quotations he makes, amply justify his language.

others, if he quit it for any disgraceful reason, as to turn pickpocket, to frequent houses of ill-fame, &c."* Lying is constantly inculcated, as a most legitimate means of self-defence against scandalous charges. "It is certain," says Caramuel, "it is a probable opinion, (*i.e.* an opinion on which one may safely act,) that it is no mortal sin to bring a false accusation for the purpose of preserving one's honour, for it is maintained by upwards of twenty grave doctors, Gaspar, Hurtado, Dicastillus, &c. Hence, if it be *not* probable, there is scarcely any one that is so, in the whole system of divinity."† Nay, not merely may lying, but murder itself, be had recourse to for this purpose: "A priest, or a monk," says Father Lamy, "is allowed to kill a calumniator, who threatens to publish scandalous crimes of their society, or of themselves, if there exist no other means of prevention."‡ Will any one say, that these maxims are exploded? They have been inculcated in recent times, and have brought forth their appropriate fruit, as the fol-

* Lett. vi. p. 78. † Lett. vii. ‡ Ibid. p. 112.

lowing case from the Foreign Quarterly Review will show:—

"In 1813, the very year before Jesuitism was formally restored, Francis Salis Riembauer, priest of Priel, in the neighbourhood of Munich, was tried, condemned, and executed, for the murder of his servant maid, Anna Maria Eichstadter, who was with child to him. Before his execution, he made public confession of the motive that induced him to commit the bloody deed. The young woman having threatened to publish his sin, 'I thought,' said he, 'of the doctrine of Father Benedict Stattler, in his *Ethica Christiana*, which holds it lawful to take away the life of another, when there exists no other way of preserving our reputation; for reputation is more valuable than life itself; and we may defend it against an attack, as we should defend ourselves against a murderer.' 'Of one or both of us,' reasoned Riembauer, 'the hour is come,' and tranquillized by the doctrine of the Jesuit, he re-entered the room, seized his victim, and completed his crime with a barbarity, the details of which we willingly pass over. 'While she lay on the ground,' said he, 'I administered to her spiritual consolation, till her feet began to quiver, and her last breath departed. I know no more of this sad story, but my deep grief and silent lamentation; and that I often since *applied* masses for her soul." "How completely," adds the Reviewer, "does this last expression reveal the idea, which this wretch had of the rites of religion, when he talks of *applying* a mass or two, as an apothecary would, of *applying* an ointment or a plaster."*

Such is Jesuitism. Such was it in the days of Pascal; such is it in the present day. About the middle of the last century, when public attention was strongly called to the subject, and the immorality of the system exposed, the Jesuits fell under a storm of popular indignation. They were driven in succession from Portugal, from France, from Spain, from Naples, and from all the Roman Catholic nations of Europe. The Pope himself was compelled to suppress the so-

* Foreign Quarterly Review. German Trials, 1831.

ciety, and 326 different publications of their writers were, by order of the parliament of Paris, in 1762, burnt by the hands of the common executioner. "Of these works, all approved by three Jesuit divines," according to the Archbishop of Malines, "17 encourage immodesty; 28 perjury; 33 theft; 36 murder; 68 regicide; 14 simony, &c." And yet, without the slightest change of the system, have the promoters of all this immorality been re-established by the Pope, as the grand defenders of the Papacy. Nay, as if this of itself were not enough to shew the favour in which Jesuitism is held at Rome, Alphonso Liguori, whose life and energies were spent in upholding those principles from which all these abominations necessarily spring, after being canonized by Pius VII., has recently been canonized a *second time*, with all pomp and splendour, by the Pope.* Thus has the Pope identified himself, and the church of which he is the head, with the wickedness of Jesuitism. It is undeniable now that

* Gaussen's Geneva and Rome, p. 14.

Jesuitism is Popery, and that Popery is Jesuitism. There was once a strong party in the French church that contended for the Gallican liberties, and for much that was good and true, in opposition to the Jesuits; but now ultramontanism is nearly as rampant there as in Italy itself. The French bishops, we are told by Michelet, even glory in being disciples of Loyola. "We are Jesuits," say they, "*all* Jesuits."* Now, Jesuitism being thus fostered and cherished by the Pope, it is impossible to doubt that he is "that Lawless One," who was to set himself above all authority, and trample on all law human and divine.†

The people of God, who should see such a system established, and the Man of sin fully revealed, were not to be left in any doubt as to his fate. If they had merely seen him sitting in the temple of God, shewing himself that he

* Michelet's Priests, Women, and Families, p. 1.

† Those who would wish to see farther proof, that the pope is indeed the "Lawless One," may consult Dr Cunningham's admirable edition of Stillingfleet, under the head "Dispensations."

was God, setting up kings, putting them down at his pleasure, and governing the world at his nod, without any intimation of his doom, they might have been in danger of sinking into despondency at the thought of his mighty power. But the Lord no sooner announces his rise, than he pronounces his sentence. He is the "Son of perdition," destined to destruction, "whom the Lord shall consume with the spirit of his mouth, and destroy (or abolish)* with the brightness of his coming." From the expression "consume† with the spirit of his mouth," some have taken up the notion that Popery would perish by a gradual consumption, that light and knowledge would more and more spread throughout Christendom, that the Man of Sin himself would be converted, and that the whole system of Papal superstition would gently and easily melt away. Alas!

"Leviathan is not so tamed."

The Bible leads us to anticipate a very different

* Καταργήσει.

† Ἀναλώσει does not properly signify "to waste away," but simply "to destroy."

doom for apostate Rome. The angel whom John saw announcing its end, took up a stone like a great millstone, and cast it into the sea, saying, "Thus with *violence* shall that great city Babylon be thrown down, and shall be found no more at all." It is not by the progress of knowledge, it is not by the Holy Spirit, that the "Lawless One" is to be consumed. It is by desolating judgments that he is to be brought low. In all the parallel texts where the same form of expression is used as that employed here, it is not reformation, but judgment that is referred to. Thus, for instance, Eliphaz speaks of the destruction of the wicked: "By the blast of God they perish; and by the breath of his nostrils are they consumed."* Isaiah, speaking of the reign of the Messiah, and perhaps referring to this very event, says: "With righteousness shall he judge the poor, and reprove with equity for the meek of the earth. He shall smite the earth with the rod of his mouth, and with the breath of his lips shall he slay the wicked."†

* Job iv. 9. † Isai. xi. 4.

And in the Apocalypse we are told: "Out of his *mouth* goeth a sharp two-edged sword, that with it he should smite the nations: and he shall rule them with a rod of iron: and he treadeth the winepress of the fierceness and wrath of Almighty God."* It is not conversion, then, but destruction that awaits apostate Rome; and therefore the voice from heaven, before her end, cries, "Come out of her, my people, that ye be not partakers of her sins, and that ye partake not of her plagues." Yes; though her excellency mount up to the heavens, and her head reach unto the clouds, "she shall be utterly burned with fire; for strong is the Lord God, which judgeth her."

> "Rome shall perish, write that word,
> In the blood that she hath spilt,
> Perish hopeless and abhorred,
> Deep in ruin as in guilt."

The question here arises, Will this judgment be inflicted by Christ in *person*, or through his ordinary providence? This is a question which

* Rev. xix. 15.

I will not venture positively to determine. When I look at the first verse of this chapter, and find Paul saying, "I beseech you, brethren, by the *coming* of our Lord Jesus Christ, and our gathering together to him," which without doubt refers to his *personal* coming, I might be inclined to think that he must refer to the same event here, when he says that the Man of Sin is "to be destroyed by the brightness of Christ's *coming*." But when I observe, on the other hand, that in the very verse that follows the present, he uses the very same term to designate the *coming* of Antichrist, which unquestionably is not a *local* or *personal* coming, but the prevalence of a system, I am led to pause before departing from the common interpretation; and the rather, because the doctrine of Christ's personal reign is encumbered with difficulties which I feel myself unable to remove. Without, therefore, speaking dogmatically, I would incline to the opinion, that while fearful judgments will be inflicted upon the head and members of the Roman church, "the brightness of Christ's coming," or in other words, the clear shining of gospel light, that shall at the same time be vouchsafed, will "abolish" every trace of the anti-christian system, and usher in the time when the knowledge of the glory of the Lord shall cover the earth as the waters cover the sea, when "men shall be blessed in Christ, when all nations shall call him blessed."

CHAPTER VI.

The Energy of Satan.
The Signs and Lying Wonders of the Man of Sin.

2 Thessalonians ii. 9.

Even him, whose coming is after the working of Satan, with all power, and SIGNS, AND LYING WONDERS.

We have here a distinct intimation, both of the real author of the apostacy, and of one of the grand engines he would make use of in promoting it.

1. The Devil is expressely declared to be the author of Popery. "The coming of the Man of Sin," says Paul, "is after the working of Satan." It was not mere human wisdom that was to be concerned in planning—not mere hu-

man agency employed in carrying out the system of antichrist. The system was to be concocted in hell, and the arch-fiend was to organize and direct its movements. Ambitious and wicked churchmen have been Satan's tools; but from the beginning he has himself been actively engaged in the management of the whole machinery of the mystery of iniquity. Nay, it is here intimated, that his chief strength would be put forth in the Apostacy. "The working of Satan," in the original, is "the energy or mighty power of Satan;" and Popery may most justly be characterized, as it has been by Cecil, as "Satan's masterpiece." As the gospel is "the power of God unto salvation," so Popery is emphatically "the power of Satan unto perdition." In leading captive the heathen, who had the mere light of reason to guide them, the enemy of souls had comparatively an easy task to perform; but after that the day-spring from on high had visited mankind—after that life and immortality had been brought to light by the gospel—after that the word of God had been preached to all nations—to envelope these nations again in worse than Pagan darkness, was a much more arduous undertaking. This was the object, to effect which, Satan addressed himself; and this, in the unsearchable wisdom of God, was he permitted to accomplish.

At the Reformation, indeed, his wonted skill seemed to desert him. He committed blunder after blunder; and his throne seemed to totter to its fall. But the defeat which Satan at that time sustained, has only been the means of showing more clearly the mighty resources which are at the command of his malignity. The deadly wound inflicted on his antichristian kingdom has been healed; and the Papacy is again instinct with even more than the ancient "energy of Satan." The spread of science, the invention of printing, the march of mind, the open Bible itself, and the thousand advantages which have raised the present age intellectually above all preceding ages, have not secured the nations of Protestant Europe against the seductions of Rome. Human wisdom has been trusted in; and human wisdom, as might have been expected, has been found no match for the subtlety of the old serpent, sharpened, as that subtlety is, by the experience of six thousand years. Philosophers are amazed at the return of obsolete and exploded superstitions; and politicians, who thought to outwit the Man of Sin, find themselves duped and helpless in his hands. The rapidity with which Popery spreads, amid all the illumination of the nineteenth century, surpasses any thing ever known before. "The growth of the Popish system," observes an able writer, "at first was a work of ages; but in the present case, it grows more in a year than it did then in half a century. It would seem as if the old sorceress had reserved this unparalleled effort of skill to the last. That she should have bewitched and enslaved the comparatively barbarous tribes of Europe in the fifth and sixth centuries, or that she should have swayed a sceptre of absolute sovereignty over the dark ages, was nothing so extraordinary. But to reconquer England, that has scoffed at the pretensions of Rome for three hundred years, to lead captive a kingdom so renowned throughout the world for its wealth and power, its intelligence and science, is an achievement that may well waken astonishment. The conquests of her youth were paltry, when compared with the triumphs of her old age. She has 'painted her face, and tired her head, and looked out at her window;' but none of the dignitaries, either in church or state, seem in the least inclined to repeat Jehu's cry, 'Throw her down.'"*

Thus does Rome triumph in England, the ancient home of the Reformation—the land so signally blessed of Heaven in times past for its adherence to Protestantism; and the wisest statesmen of the day, as the world counts wisdom, instead of resisting her encroachments, are fain to crouch at her feet. But how strikingly does this illustrate the word of God! how clearly does it prove that antichrist is upheld

* Dr Bates of Glasgow. Introduction to Macleod on the Revelation.

by "the mighty power of Satan!" It was the knowledge of the Satanic influence pervading the system of Rome, that made our ancestors dread it so much—that made John Knox, for instance, declare, that he would rather hear of an army of 20,000 men landed on his native shores, than that one mass should be again celebrated in Scotland. The Reformers knew well the enemy they had to contend with. They knew, that as the mystery of godliness is "God manifest in the flesh," so the mystery of iniquity is the Devil with all his hellish craft embodied in the Papacy.

2. One of the means by which Satan was to introduce apostacy into the Christian church, was false miracles. Antichrist was to "come with signs and lying wonders;" and the Church of Rome has ever made use of these, as among the approved weapons of her warfare. In the very earliest ages of the church, as false doctrine spread, false miracles spread along with it. The monks and hermits, who set up for paragons of superhuman virtue, tried to raise

their own credit, and the credit of that system of will-worship and asceticism which they introduced, by laying claim to superhuman powers. And in exact proportion as men departed from the faith, and the light of the gospel was obscured, did the pretensions to miraculous powers increase. This any one may be convinced of who reads consecutively the ecclesiastical histories of Eusebius, Socrates, and Evagrius. Eusebius, who details the history of the first three centuries, with the exception of the apostolic miracles, which are admitted on all hands to be divine, says comparatively little of the supernatural pretensions of the Christians. Not that false miracles were then unknown; but they were not yet so deeply inwoven into the ecclesiastical system as to require to be much obtruded on the reader. In the narrative of Socrates, which includes the next 150 years, they become more and more frequent; and in the History of Evagrius, who brings us down to the end of the sixth century, when saint-worship was thoroughly established, and the Man of sin was just about to be revealed, we can hardly open a page that is not full of such "lying wonders." Throughout the dark ages that followed, the wonder-working powers of antichrist had full scope for their development.

Many of the miracles, indeed, in the lives of the Romish saints, are mere fabrications and fictions; and never had any other foundation than the invention of the writer. "The Golden Legend," says Ludovicus Vives, himself a Papist, "was written by a man of an iron face and a leaden heart, and is full of most shameless lies."* Rome has so managed matters that she may always have abundance of this sort of miracles. While it is indispensable to canonization that the working of miracles be alleged, no saint can be canonized, except in rare cases where money is all-powerful, till he have been dead for at least fifty years. The holy fathers pretend to go through the form of a scrutiny into the evidence of these miracles, in

* Lud. Viv. De causs. corrupt. art. tom. i. lib. 2. p. 371. Basil, 1555.

circumstances in which that scrutiny must be a mere mockery. How unlike the miraculous pretensions of the apostles, which were openly asserted in the midst of those who could personally have disputed them,— (if to dispute them had been possible!) The Romish miracles are examined only after all are dead and gone, who knew any thing about the matter. Yet even with all this in his favour, the Man of Sin has been *convicted* of stamping with his infallible authority, miracles that never had any shadow of foundation. In the case of St Ignatius Loyola this is most evident. The first who undertook to write the life of the father and founder of Jesuitism was his disciple Ribadeneira, who, while he states that he had been *an eyewitness and admirer of his holy life from his youth*, so far from asserting that Ignatius wrought miracles, expresses his astonishment that so holy a man *had* NOT *the power of working miracles*. This was when Loyola had been dead only fifteen years, and when the idea of laying a foundation for the canonization of the patron saint of hypocrisy and immorality had not entered his mind. Time, however, rolls away: the glory of the order requires that its founder should be canonized; and now, at the distance of fifty-five years from Loyola's death, and forty years from the publication of the first edition of his life, this same Ribadeneira puts forth an abridgement, in which, *for the first time*, he declares that Ignatius had the power of working miracles! Such a statement, in such circumstances evidently bears on the face of it marks of fabrication. Thousands of the stories of miracles to be found in the lives of the Romish saints had unquestionably no higher origin. They were not, properly speaking, "lying wonders," but simply "lies."

But Popery, nevertheless, has had false miracles in abundance, which imposed even upon those who witnessed them. Its priests, monopolizing for centuries all the knowledge that was, and keeping the people in abject ignorance, have successfully deluded them into the belief of their supernatural powers. This they have done in two ways, either by dexterously contriving matters, so as to make it appear that what happened in the natural course of God's providence, was done in direct answer to their prayers, or by juggling tricks and downright impostures. In the first case, suppose an epidemic prevails in a city; they watch the progress of the scourge; they acquaint themselves accurately with its ravages; they make it a point to ascertain the moment it has reached its height. Immediately, the aids of superstition are invoked: the Virgin or some favourite saint is publicly supplicated to arrest the pestilence: the disease subsides, and the saint and his ministers are rewarded and blessed for their seasonable interference. Such, without doubt, was the way in which "the miraculous image" of the Virgin arrested the progress of the cholera at Ancona.* Such is the approved method by which a conflagration is checked in Roman Catholic countries, and power and wealth secured to the priests. Of

* Referred to in Free Assembly 1846, by Rev. Andrew Gray of Perth.

such a mode of extinguishing a fire as practised at Granada, while he was there, Inglis gives the following lively description in his Tour in Spain. "The noise," says he, "still continued, and the fire not being speedily got under by human efforts, stronger measures were resorted to. The sound of bells and trumpets was exchanged for the song of monks. I heard the monotonous hum from several quarters; lights in long lines were seen approaching; and soon one procession, and then another headed by a silver Virgin, or a wooden saint, crossed the Plaza; and all the while the streets were paraded by single friars, each tinkling a little bell and crying aloud, "Holy Mary! Blessed Virgin, save this city!" This proved effectual, for the fire was subdued before morning. I need scarcely add, that before the procession issued from the convent, a hint had been received that the fire would speedily be got under—and who can be surprised that the brethren of St Francis and St Dominick should seize so excellent an opportunity of publishing a miracle?"*

* Tour in Spain in 1830, vol. ii.

This is one way in which Rome has deluded the people. But it is by the other, by her juggleries and impostures, that she has especially earned for herself the character given her in the Apocalypse, of deceiving the nations "by her sorceries." Individuals in her pay have been trained to counterfeit disease, that she might have the merit of instantaneously healing them. Of this kind was the last miracle publicly attempted by the supporters of the Papacy in Scotland. To prop their tottering cause, public notice was given that on a certain day they would put the truth of their religion to the test, by curing a young man who had been born blind, at the chapel of our Lady of Loretto, near Musselburgh. The appointed day came; a crowd collected to witness the miracle; and there too was produced the young man, apparently stone blind, accompanied by a procession of monks. The Virgin was solemnly invoked, and immediately, to the astonishment of the spectators, the blind youth recovered his sight. There was one among the crowd, however, who suspected some deception. Colville of Cleish, who ardently supported the Reformation, found means, after the ceremonial of the day was over, to bring the young man to his house, locked him up in his room, and drew from him the whole secret. The lad confessed that when a boy he had learnt the trick of turning up the white of his eyes, and keeping them in that position, so as to appear blind; that the monks, becoming aware of this, had first sent him out to act the part of a blind beggar, and then when the public were familiarized with his appearance in that capacity, had brought him forward to exhibit in him a proof of their wonder-working powers. "To confirm his narrative," says M'Crie, "the lad 'played his payvie before Colville, by flypping up the lid of his eyes and casting up the white, to perfection. Upon this Colville exposed the whole story, and made the young man repeat it at the cross of Edinburgh, to the confusion of the whole fraternity of monks and friars; who would, no doubt, have wreaked their vengeance upon their former tool, and made him blind enough, had not Cleish stood beside him with his drawn sword, placed him when he had done on his own horse, and carried him off to Fife."

The impostures which were practised on the benighted people during the dark ages would hardly be credible, if we had not indubitable evidence of the facts. "In those days," says Bishop Jewell, "idols could go on foot, roods could speak, bells could ring alone, images could come down and light their own candles; dead stocks could sweat and bestir themselves; they could turn their eyes, they could move their hands, they could open their mouths, they could set bones and knit sinews; they could heal the sick, and raise the dead. These miracles were contrivances and subtleties, and indeed no miracles. The tongues by which they spake, the strings and wires by which they moved their faces and their hands, and all the rest of their treachery, have been disclosed."* Nor have these impostures been brought to light only by Protestants. The feuds subsisting between the different orders in the Romish Church, have helped not a

* British Reformers, Jewell. p. 246.

little to unveil the nakedness of the whole system, and expose the lying wonders of the Man of Sin. About the year 1509, an acrimonious controversy was carried on in the city of Berne in Switzerland, between the Franciscans and Dominicans, about the immaculate conception of the Virgin. The warfare was waged for some time with doubtful success; but at length to the astonishment of the faithful, it seemed fairly determined by the Virgin herself. One day, on some solemn occasion, when the worshippers were assembled in crowds in the chapel of the Dominicans, a prodigy appeared. All eyes are arrested by seeing the image of the Virgin in tears. While they gaze, their wonder is raised to the highest pitch. The image of the infant Jesus is heard to speak: "Mother, why do you weep?" "How can I but weep," replies the Virgin, "when men attribute that honour to me which belongs to you alone?" The Virgin herself thus repudiates the idea of her immaculate conception; and the Dominicans triumph. Their triumphing, however, is only for a moment. Their adversaries, the Franciscans, are not to be so foiled. Knowing what they would do in a like case themselves, they suspect some cheat. They have their wits about them, and by means of a deserter from the Franciscan convent, the whole trick is disclosed. It is discovered that there was a communication between the images and an adjoining cell by means of a tube, and that a friar stationed in that cell, and speaking through the tube, had been the author of the miracle, that so astonished the multitude. Bishop Burnett informs us, in his book of travels, that at the time when he visited Berne, the hole through which the friar spoke, was still to be seen.*

In recent times, when light has abounded, the Roman Catholic priests have been rather more chary of their miracles; but they have never failed to have recourse to them whenever they thought they might safely do so. Even the Jansenists, notwithstanding their superior morality and decided leaning to evangelism, seem, in this

* Bishop Hurd's Rites and Ceremonies, p. 131.

respect, to have been deeply infected with the poison of Antichrist, and to have thought it quite legitimate to meet fraud with counter-fraud. The miracle wrought by the "Holy Thorn" on Marguerite Perier, the niece of the illustrious Pascal, was beyond doubt of the same nature as the other lying wonders of Romanism; and it seems certain that that which gave the death-blow to Jansenism in France, was not so much the power of hostile princes, and the bulls of anathematising popes, as the exposure made by its adversaries, the Jesuits, of the frauds practised by its adherents, who resorted for miraculous cures to the tomb of the Abbé Paris.

The pretensions to miraculous powers on the part of Roman Catholics of late years, have been decidedly on the increase. The miracles of Maria Mörl and Domenica Lazzari that gained so much eclat in Austria, and which were so confidently vouched by Lord Shrewsbury, have been recently repeated in Ireland under the patronage of Father Foley, a priest in Youghal. But what was hailed in Papal Austria, as a signal proof of the miraculous interference of heaven, when subjected to the keen scrutiny of Irish Protestants, has been so thoroughly proved to be an arrant cheat, that the leading Romanists themselves have been compelled to disavow those who were concerned in it. Yet in spite of all the exposures that have been made of the "pious frauds" of the Romish Church, she asserts at this moment as strongly as ever she did in her palmiest days, her possession of miraculous powers. The following extract from Mumford's Catholic Scripturist, recommended by Bishop Murdoch of Glasgow, only in 1841, as a "work of undoubted orthodoxy," may show how absurd is the idea now adopted by many, that popery is changed and reformed:—"Let no man think that miracles now cease. All England knows, that our kings, by touching with certain ceremonies, cured the king's evil; and all France knows, their kings do so to this day. The first for St Edward's sake; the other for St Lewis's. . . . . Believe to find no true belief where there are no true miracles." Miracles then, on the authority of this "work of undoubted orthodoxy," are still, according to Rome, the marks of the true church. What kind of miracles those were which were wrought for the sake of St Edward and St Lewis, no intelligent reader need be told. But here we have Rome, out of her own mouth, convicted of bearing the mark of the Man of Sin, "whose coming was to be after the working of Satan, with power, and signs, and lying wonders."

CHAPTER VII.

Conclusion.
The Strong Delusions accompanying the Apostacy.

2 THESSALONIANS ii. 10–12.

"And with all deceivableness of unrighteousness in them that perish; because they received not the love of the truth, that they might be saved. And for this cause God shall send them STRONG DELUSION, that they should believe a lie; that they all might be damned who believed not the truth, but had pleasure in unrighteousness.

THE subtlety of Satan is great; the means, which he employs for deceiving the nations and bringing them under bondage to Antichrist, are well fitted to accomplish that end; but there is another element to be considered in accounting for the spread of popery, than any that has yet come before us. It is the result of judicial blindness and infatuation. The chief reason that Anti-christian error ravaged the church at first, is not to be found in the weakness of men's minds, in the mere *natural* depravity of the human heart, or the cunning devices of Satan; but in the fact, that for their ingratitude and misimprovement of privilege, "God had given them up to a reprobate mind." The Gospel is God's best and chiefest gift to the world. It demands the affections of the heart; it is worthy of them. If, therefore, when it is proclaimed to a people, they do not surrender their hearts to it, it is at their peril. Now the great multitude of professors in the Christian church soon began to hold the truth in unrighteousness. They wished, at one and the same time, to serve God and mammon. They made the doctrines of Christianity matters of barren speculation. While the truth entered their heads and played about their imaginations, they allowed it not to influence their lives and conduct. And thus they became the prey of Antichrist; "Because they received not the love of the truth that they might be saved, *for this cause* God sent them strong delusion, that they should believe a lie." Without bearing this in mind, it will hardly be possible to account for the firm hold which popery maintains on its votaries. It makes larger draughts on their credulity than any other form of idolatry, than even Paganism itself ever did. What, for instance, can be compared with the outrageous and irrational dogma of transubstantiation? "I have taken some pains," said Sheffield, duke of Buckingham, when pressed by the Popish priests of James VII. to turn Papist, "I have taken some pains to believe in God, who made the world, and all men in it; but I shall not be easily persuaded that man is quits, and makes God again." But this substantially every Papist believes. He believes that his priest, by the pronunciation of four Latin words, converts a piece of bread into the body and blood, along with the soul and divinity, of our Lord Jesus Christ.* And

* "He that created me," says Cardinal Biel, "gave me, if it be lawful to tell, power to create himself." Biel Lect. IV.

this he believes in defiance of the plainest evidence of his senses to the contrary. His senses, sight, and touch, and taste, and smell, all combine to assure him that the bread remains bread exactly as it was before; but, nevertheless, on the bare word of his priest, he believes, that after consecration, not a particle of bread is left, but that the Lord of glory himself is literally present before him, under the form and appearance of the wafer! A belief such as this can spring from nothing but the most monstrous delusion.

The circumstances, too, in which many nominal Protestants in recent times, have allowed themselves either to be carried over to Popery, or to give their strength to the beast, forcibly illustrate the language of the prediction. With regard to the former, what, for instance, could be a more gross delusion, than that which was exhibited in the case of Antony Ulric, the late duke of Brunswick? This prince had lived the most of his life in the profession of Protestantism. In his old age he became Papist, and published his reasons for doing so. These were no fewer than "fifty;" but the last, and that which weighed with him above all, was this, that all "the Catholics to whom he spoke on the subject of his conversion, assured him, that if he was damned for embracing the Catholic faith, *they were ready to answer for him at the day of judgment, and take his damnation upon themselves:*" "an assurance," adds the duke, "I could never extort from the ministers of any sect, in case I should live and die in their religion; whence I inferred that the Roman Catholic faith was built upon a better foundation than any of those sects that have divided from it!!" Could any one draw such an inference, could any one stake his salvation upon such a hazard, but one who was "given up to strong delusion to believe a lie"?

The way in which Mr Pitt persuaded himself that it was right and fit for a Protestant government to endow the Popish college of Maynooth, bears equally palpable marks of judicial infatuation. The opponents of that measure maintained, on the testimony, not only of history, but of God's infallible Word, that the emissaries of Rome taught immoral and anti-social doctrines, and in particular, were distinguished for "speaking lies in hypocrisy, having their consciences seared with a hot iron." Mr Pitt was bent upon carrying his point. How was this argument to be disposed of? Did he listen to the dictates of Scripture? Did he carefully enquire whether these things were so? No; he treated the Scriptural argument with contempt; and although one of the main charges against Rome was, that it trampled upon truth whenever its interests were thereby to be promoted, he applied to sundry professors of divinity in the universities of that very apostate Church, such as Louvain, Alcala, &c., to resolve the question, whether it was true that they held it lawful to break faith with heretics or not. The government of Great Britain were at that time guilty of the very crime of which the king of Israel was guilty, when, despising the oracle of God, he sent to inquire of the god of Ekron, and drew down upon himself the prophetic denunciation of the Tishbite: "Forasmuch as thou hast sent messengers to enquire of Baalzebub, the god of Ekron, is it not because there is not a God in Israel, to enquire of his word? Therefore, thus saith the Lord, thou shalt not come down from off that bed on which thou art gone up, but shalt surely die." To me it seems that at that very period, the constitution of this once Protestant country, which had long before been enfeebled by the policy of irreligious statesmen, received an immedicable wound. Having set at nought the wisdom of God, it was a righteous thing in Him, whom our rulers had contemned, to turn their wisdom into foolishness, and to give them up to a gross and palpable delusion. And what infatuation could be greater than to receive as decisive of the question, the testimony of men whose own veracity was impeached by the very enquiry that was put to them? "May we heretics implicitly rely on the word of a Papist?" said Mr Pitt to the Popish professors. "Yes, most assuredly," replied the grave and reverend seigniors.* Mr Pitt and his government were satisfied, and that course of policy was openly and avowedly entered upon, that has left very few traces of Protestantism in the British constitution.

And do not the circumstances in which the recent favours were heaped on the priests of Rome, demonstrate that the same judicial infatuation still operates on men in power in full force? What is there in the present doings of that apostate church to give the slightest colour to the plea that the persecuting spirit of Popery is changed? Is it the eight months' imprisonment of Dr Kalley in the dungeon of Funchal for speaking to the Portuguese on religion in his own house;† the sentence of death pronounced on Maria Joaquina for holding it unlawful to worship the Virgin; the condemnation of Ensign Maclachlan to six months' imprisonment

* See Note I.

† While this is passing through the press, Dr Kalley, and some hundreds of his converts have been obliged to flee from Madeira, to save their lives from the fury of a Popish rabble evidently connived at by the authorities.

in Malta, for *accidentally* dropping a few walnut shells out of his window into the street, while the host was passing; the renewed cruelty and oppression practised on the unoffending Waldenses, or the devastation carried by fire and sword over the lovely isles of the South Sea for their adherence to God's word and to Protestantism? All these things have taken place within the last few years, and they are known to the whole world. Providence seems to have so ordered it, that the real character of Popery should be more unequivocally developed at this moment, than it has been for more than a century past. And yet at this very time the leading statesmen of the age are firmly persuaded that the only way to promote the peace and prosperity of Protestant Britain is to give power and emolument to that blood-thirsty church. Nay, though Popery be at present revealed in all its nakedness, multitudes brought up in the bosom of a church long regarded as the bulwark of Protestantism, seem rushing as fast as they can into the embraces of the Mother of Harlots. Amid all the boasted science of the age, Protestants are lighting wax candles at noonday, bowing down before wooden crosses, "turning to the east when reading prayers, and to the south when reading lessons;"* and not a few are going over bodily to Rome. How is this to be accounted for? How comes it that Popery spreads with such unprecedented rapidity at the present day? The language of the prediction before us furnishes the answer. There had been a revival of evangelical religion. Under the ministry of such men as Romaine and Berridge, and Newton and Scott, the gospel was powerfully and faithfully preached and pressed on the consciences and hearts of men. But while the *name* of Evangelism became fashionable, its paramount claims were practically set at nought by the vast majority of those who professed it. The consequence was what the Spirit of God had denounced: "Because they received not the love of the truth, that they might be saved, for this cause God

* According to the Bishop of London's advice, in his famous charge.

hath sent them strong delusion that they should believe a lie."

There are many who think, when they hear of the revival of Popery in the south, and of the probability of its spread throughout the land, that there is no fear of *them*, that they are too rational, too enlightened to be in any danger of being carried away by its gross superstitions. But it is very possible that such may find themselves mistaken. If they trust only in their own wisdom, they are leaning on a broken reed. Many of those in England who are now mad upon their idols, were, only ten or fiften years ago, as little likely, to all appearance, to become the slaves of superstition, as those who now flatter themselves on their imaginary security, and would have laughed to scorn any who at that time should have told them that they would ever turn, what by this time they have actually become. Dr Pusey himself began his career as a Rationalist.

But it may not be amiss for those who think

themselves so wise in matters of religion, to examine and see if they be indeed as rational as they suppose themselves to be. If they deal faithfully with their own souls, it may be found that most of those who look upon themselves as so completely beyond the reach of Popish delusion, have only a name to live, while they are dead, and a form of godliness while they are destitute of the power of it. If this be so, what claims can they have to the character of rational men?

They give to the living God such a service as could reasonably be offered only to a dead idol. Though he is a spirit, and requires that those who worship him should worship him in spirit and in truth, their spirits are not at all engaged in his service. In the closet, in the family, in the sanctuary, they draw near to him with their mouth and honour him with their lips, while their hearts are far from him. Their religion is mere ceremony. "They worship they know not what." They pour their prayers to vacancy; to the empty air, or to the blue sky; and when the routine is gone through they are satisfied. Is this rational?

They admit that it is in God they live and move and have their being, that his favour is life, that his frown is death, that he can in a moment dash them in pieces as a potter's vessel; and yet, they fear to offend any one rather than him; they dread the displeasure of a man that shall die, and of the son of man that shall be made as grass, and forget the Lord their Maker. Is this consistent with reason?

They profess to believe that the Son of the Highest left his eternal throne, was born in a stable and laid in a manger; was despised and rejected of men; was tempted of devils, and expired on the accursed tree, under the hidings of his Father's countenance, that they might escape the damnation of hell and inherit eternal life; and yet they feel no constraining love to him, no devotion, no gratitude; nay, they hardly ever think of him. Is this worthy of an intelligent creature?

They know that they are strangers and pilgrims here,—that this world is not their home,—that they must soon go the way of all the earth; and yet, while careful about the interests of this short and precarious life, they make no provision for the life to come. They know that it is not only appointed unto men once to die, but after this the judgment; and yet they live as if their souls were destined to go down to the dust with the beasts that perish, and as if it were certain that they would never be called to give account of the deeds done in the body.

Now, what pretensions to sense or reason can those have who live thus? They are guilty of the most blind and infatuated conduct. And such are the great mass of nominal Protestants. What wonder, then, if at any time they shall be entangled in the meshes of Popery? They only pass from one form of delusion to another; and it is but a slight step that they need to take. And when the time comes that shall try them that dwell on all the earth, assuredly it will not be mere intellectual light that shall hinder them from being carried away by the absurdities of Rome. "All that dwell on the earth shall worship the beast, whose names were not written in the Lamb's book of life from the foundation of the world."

And what is to be the consequence of this judicial blindness? It is perdition. This is unequivocally declared. "God," says the apostle, "shall send them strong delusion, that they should believe a lie, that they all might be damned who believed not the truth, but had pleasure in unrighteousness." Those who think lightly of Popery, as a form of Christianity, should remember this. If the Gospel be true, the religion of Rome is a God-dishonouring, soul-ruining system. Whatever God may do with individuals, who never had an opportunity of knowing better, he will, beyond doubt, execute his wrath upon those who have had the truth of God in their offer, and have wilfully cast it from them, that they might receive the devil's lie. In the long dreary ages of darkness, when Popery lorded it over the world, there were, there is every reason to believe, not a few hidden ones, even in the Roman pale, who, along with much error, nevertheless had such a glimmering of the saving truth as kept their souls in vital union with Jesus Christ. "It is with false doctrine," says good old Hugh Latimer, "like as it is with fire. The nature of the fire is to burn and consume; so the nature of false doctrine is to condemn, to bring to everlasting ruin. But yet for all that, there have been many things in the fire that have not been burned; to instance only the three children that were cast by Nebuchadnezzar into the burning fiery furnace. Though the fire, of its own nature, would have consumed them, yet through the power of God, the strength of the fire was vanquished, the men were preserved, and not an hair of their heads perished. Even so it is with Popery, with false doctrine; the nature of it is to consume, to bring to everlasting sorrow; yet let us hope, that our forefathers were not damned, for God had many ways to preserve them from perishing."* Doubtless there is consolation in the thought here presented; but those saved in such circumstances were saved as by miracle. There is nothing in this to warrant any one to look upon it as a light thing, to leave the Gospel of the grace of God now purely preached, and to embrace the superstition and idolatry of Rome in its stead. Those who in such circumstances draw back from a profession of the Protestant faith, have too much reason to fear that they draw back unto perdition: "It had been better for them not to have known the way of truth, than having known it, to turn from the holy commandment."

It is this view of the matter that makes it so sad, to see the tide setting in so strongly in the direction of Rome. It is this that ought to make every man jealous over himself with a godly jealousy. It is this that ought to arouse the people of God at least, to do what they can

* Latimer's Sermon on the Christian Walk, abridged.

to prevent the pestilence from spreading, and to labour, and wrestle, and pray, that those who are dear to them may be preserved from the delusions that are coming thick and fast upon the world. The greatest exertions that can now be made, may not perhaps avail to prevent the restoration of the Papal dominion in these realms. But the faithfulness of those who do exert themselves, will not, on that account, be in vain. Their zeal may be blessed for the salvation of many souls; and, at all events, when the vials of God's wrath are poured out upon Babylon, having kept themselves pure from her sins, they will not be "partakers of her plagues."

NOTES.

Note A.

Papists will have it, that Peter was the *rock*, on which the church was to be built. Neither the language employed in the text, nor the nature of the case, admit of this interpretation. Our Lord, in the original, carefully distinguishes between Peter and the rock, using one word to denote the Apostle, and another to denote the foundation of His church. "Thou art (πέτρος) a stone; and on this (πέτρᾳ) rock, will I build my church." The two *words* here used are different, and the *ideas* are essentially different. A rock is one thing, and a stone is quite another. A rock is fixed and stable; a stone is moveable. The character of Peter, even as recorded in the very chapter where this saying occurs, shows that however fit he was as "a living stone," for forming a part in that great spiritual temple, which Christ came into the world to rear, he was very far indeed from being firm and immoveable as a rock; for scarcely had he witnessed the good confession, which our Lord commended, when he was again moved away from his stedfastness, and drew down upon himself the rebuke, "Get thee behind me, Satan, for thou art an offence unto me." What, then, was the *rock* on which the church was to be built! Beyond doubt, it was the Lord himself, whom Peter had just confessed as "the Christ, the Son of the Living God." The term *rock* is exclusively applied in Scripture to God. "That rock," says Paul, "was Christ." "He is the rock," says Moses, "his work is perfect." "Thou art my rock," says David. Nor is this a modern interpretation, devised by Protestants in opposition to Rome. The ancient fathers, Cyprian, Cyril, Jerome, and Augustine, held the same opinion. "It was not said to Peter," says the last mentioned, "thou art the rock, but thou art Peter. The rock was Christ, whom Peter confessed."—*Aug. Retract.* i. 21.

Note B.

The quotations given in the text, showing the blasphemous homage paid by Roman Catholics to the Virgin, are truly revolting to every pious mind. It is a lamentable fact, however, that the British public is rapidly getting reconciled to such idolatrous sentiments; and thatwhich would have utterly shocked our fathers, even of the last generation, is now not only endured, but applauded by thousands, who call themselves Protestants. In proof of this, I need only refer to the crowds that recently flocked night after night to the London theatres, to hear Rossini's *Stabat Mater;* and to the rapturous encomiums bestowed by professedly Protestant journals on that "Hymn of adoration to the Virgin." That the reader may see how fallen is the Protestantism of England, I give the three following stanzas from the English version of the hymn in question:—

O Holy Mother, so ordain
And work in me, that every pain
  He suffered pierce my heart.
In all his pangs, who deigned to die
For me, O let me ever try
  With thee to bear my part.

Virgin, above all virgins blest,
O turn not thou from my request,
  Let me thy grief sustain.
Grant me my Saviour's death to bear,
With thee his holy passion share,
  And treasure all his pain.

All that he suffered let me feel,
May love for him my soul with zeal
  To bear his cross inspire.
Thus kindly, with love's holy power,
Do THOU, at that last dreadful hour,
  Screen me from God's just ire.

The hymn from which the above is taken is stated, on good authority, to be a favourite at present in the higher circles of fashion. That this should be the case is an ill omen for our country.

Note C.

There are certain cases in which the Popish priests are *enjoined* to lie, and deliberately to add perjury to lying, as the following extract from Dens will show:—

ON THE SEAL OF CONFESSION.

Q. What is the seal of Sacramental Confession?

A. It is the obligation or duty of concealing those things which are learned from Sacramental Confession.

Q. Can a case be given in which it is lawful to break the Sacramental Seal?

A. It cannot, although the life or safety of man depended thereon, or even the destruction of the commonwealth.....

Q. What answer, then, ought a confessor to give when questioned concerning a truth which he knows from Sacramental Confession only?

A. He ought to answer that he does not know it, and if it be necessary, CONFIRM THE SAME BY AN OATH.

Objection. It is in no case lawful to tell a lie, but that confessor would be guilty of a lie because he knows the truth, therefore, &c.

Answer. I deny the minor, because such a confessor is interrogated as a man, and considered as a man; but now he does not know that truth as a man, *though he knows it as God!!—Dens*, vol. vi. p. 118.

Note D.

The idea of an infidel Antichrist has been somewhat

encouraged by the rendering of our authorised version: "who opposeth and exalteth himself above all that is called God, and is worshipped." As the words here stand, the "opposition" of the Man of sin may seem to be directed against all religion, false and true alike. But as this would make the prophecy inconsistent with itself, and would altogether remove the "*mystery*" from that system of "iniquity," of which he is the head, so there is not the least necessity in the *original*, for such a translation. 'Ο ἀντικειμενος, rendered in the common version, "who opposeth," though strictly speaking a participle, occurs in the New Testament repeatedly as a noun. In this sense, it is found in the following passages. 1 Cor. xvi. 9. "For a great door and effectual is opened to me, and there are many *adversaries*" (και ἀντικειμενοι πολλοι). Philipp. i. 28. "And in nothing terrified by your adversaries," (ὑπο των ἀντικειμενων). 1 Tim. v. 14. I will therefore, that the younger women marry, bear children, guide the house, give none occasion to the adversary (τῳ ἀντικειμενῳ) to speak reproachfully.' It was in this sense that almost all the early translators rendered it in the passage before us. Of the six English versions in Bagster's Hexapla, including the Rhemish, *all* except the authorised version render it by the noun "adversary." Erasmus, Luther, and Diodati, translate it in the very same way. Now, taking it in this way, the whole verse will run thus:—"And that Man of sin be revealed, the Son of perdition, the adversary, even exalting himself above all that is called God," &c.

Note E.

Cardinal Baronius, in his Annals of the Church, is evidently exceedingly puzzled what to say about the letters of Pope Gregory on the subject of the "universal bishop." The nature of his work will not allow him altogether to pass them without notice; but he takes care to make no allusion to the passage in which Gregory declares, that "whoever either calleth himself universal priest, or desireth so to be called, is the forerunner of Antichrist." The passages, however, which he *does* quote give him sufficient trouble; and his attempts to explain them away, are of the most futile description. All the strong language which Gregory uses on the subject, he resolves into a mere excess of humility: "Non egit," says he, "ipsâ summâ, quâ pollebat, apostolicâ auctoritate, sed Christianâ humilitate, se deprimens, ut jacentem erigeret, ac deorsum humilians, ut lapsum in profundum, sursum sublevaret, qui se tollendo ceciderat." "He did not act in this instance with that supreme apostolic authority with which he was invested, but with Christian humility he lowered himself, that by so doing he might raise up him who through ambition had so grievously fallen." It would be a strange kind of "Christian humility," indeed, which would lead any one to denounce that title, which belonged to him by divine right, and which he and his predecessors had always borne, as Baronius maintains was the case with the title of universal bishop, as "a new and profane title," as a "perverse name," which he who coveted after, showed that "he was inspired by the spirit of him who fell by proudly aspiring to an equality with God"! Gregory the Great was not remarkable for his humility at any rate; and those who would gain for him the character of humility in this way, can only do so at the expense of his veracity. He expressly declares that "none of his predecessors ever consented to use this ungodly name," and that the name of universal bishop "had been offered them in the council of Chalcedon, but had been peremptorily refused." Baronius, indeed, brings one or two expressions of different Popes which might seem to contradict this; but on examination, it will be found that he has recourse to a mere verbal quibble. Pope Leo, for instance, long before Gregory's time, had subscribed himself "bishop of the universal church:" "Leo, Romae et universalis Catholicaeque ecclesiae, Episcopus." But universal bishop" is one thing, and "bishop of the Catholic and universal church" is another. Pope Leo by this title claimed *no authority* over the universal church, but simply showed thereby that he *belonged* to it, in opposition to the heretics who had separated from it. The other expression which Baronius quotes, is used in exactly the same sense.

Note F.

It need hardly be said, that Papal infallibility is alike unscriptural and unfounded. Not to mention, that one Pope has again and again directly contradicted another

Pope in matters of faith, and that, too, when speaking *ex cathedra*, their attempts to determine what is Scripture, have presented their pretensions in this respect in the most ridiculous point of view. If Papal infallibility was necessary in any case, it was surely most necessary to give a correct and authentic copy of the Scriptures; but here they have failed most egregiously. "Of all literary blunders," says D'Israeli, in his Curiosities of Literature, "none equalled that of the Vulgate, by Sixtus V.* His Holiness carefully superintended every sheet as it passed through the press; and to the amazement of the world, the work remained without a rival,—it swarmed with errata! A multitude of scraps were printed to paste over the erroneous passages, in order to give the true text. The book makes a whimsical appearance with these patches, and the heretics exulted in this demonstration of papal infallibility! The copies were called in, and violent attempts made to suppress it; a few, however, still remain for the raptures of the Biblical collectors. Not long ago, the Bible of Sixtus V. fetched above sixty guineas,—not too much for a mere book of blunders!" This Bible of Pope Sixtus had a bull prefixed to the first volume, in which the editorial Pontiff, "of his certain knowledge, and fulness of apostolical power," decreed that "this was to be held as the only authentic edition of the Vulgate," forbidding in all time coming the publication of any edition that should vary in any respect from his, under the penalty of incurring "the wrath of Almighty God,

* The Vulgate is the authorised standard of God's word among Roman Catholics.

and his blessed apostles, Peter and Paul." This was a sufficiently formidable anathema; nevertheless Pope Clement VIII., who was not less infallible than his predecessor, only two years afterwards, published a new edition, differing from that of Sixtus, in no fewer than 2000 passages!

Note G.

Puseyism, on the subject of the Confessional, has evidently studied deeply in the school of the Mystery of iniquity. In proof of this statement, let the reader peruse the following note to a sermon preached, 7th April 1844, by the Rev. P. Cheyne, before Bishop Skinner and the clergy of the diocese of Aberdeen, and published at their request:—" What man is *fit* to be judge in his own case? Who is competent to guide himself through all the doubts and snares which beset his way? Again, looking to the case of the clergy, how can they be called '*spiritual guides*?' for what do they know about the real state of the souls committed to their charge? In what way can they guide those of whose difficulties and trials, sins and weaknesses, they are totally ignorant? If there be one circumstance in our position as priests more intensely painful than another, it is this:—that we have the cure of souls, without the possibility of discharging it effectually; for nothing *can* be effectual, but that which will enable us to deal with individuals *one by one*. I must therefore express my deep conviction, founded upon reflection, observation, and experience, that nothing but the revival of *confession*, under its *sacramental sanctity*, can enable the church to act as the true mother and guide of God's children."—*Sermon of the Rev. P. Cheyne*, p. 26.

Note H.

The extent to which the Confessional has been employed for purposes of licentiousness, and the hopelessness of every attempt to remedy the evil, may be judged of from the following extract from "Edgar's Variations of Popery," page 528.

"The measureless intemperance of the Spanish clergy appears in the history of sacerdotal and monkish SOLICITATION in that kingdom. This became so prevalent as to demand pontifical interposition. Its notoriety challenged the interference of Pius, Clement, Gregory, Alexander, and Benedict, who issued their bulls against this kind of seduction. The publication of the Papal enactments showed the extent of the evil. The execution of the Roman mandates was consigned to the inquisitors, who summoned the attendance at the holy office, of all that could inform against the guilty. The terror of the inquisition commanded obedience. Maids and matrons, of the nobility and peasantry, of every rank and situation, crowded to the inquisition. Modesty and shame induced many to go veiled. The alarm awakened jealousy in the mind of many husbands. The fair informers in Seville alone, were, according to Gonsalvus and Llorente, so numerous, that all the inquisitors, and twenty notaries, were insufficient in thirty days, to take their depositions. Thirty additional days had three several times to be appointed for the reception of informations. But the multitude of criminals, the jealousy of husbands, and the odium which the discovery threw on auricular confession and the popish priesthood, caused the sacred tribunal *to quash the prosecution, and to consign the depositions to oblivion.*"

The work, from which the above is taken, is a work of great value, and immense learning and research. In one instance, however, that has come under my notice, the author, by trusting too implicitly to Romish quotations from the Fathers, has allowed himself to be led astray. He speaks as if Theodorus, or Heliodorus of Tricca, who first introduced the obligation of single life into the church, had composed his piece, called "Ethiopics," with the view of inculcating asceticism, and proscribing the marriage of the clergy; and he gives Socrates and Nicephorus as his leading authorities for the assertion. Now, it may be true that the Popish author Mendoza, to whom he also refers, may represent the matter in this light, to veil the early licentiousness of Heliodorus; but there is nothing in either of the two ancients to warrant the statement. Socrates (as the reader may have seen, page 32,) expressly calls the work an "amorous work," and Nicephorus says, that "Heliodorus was ordered in synod to burn those *amatory books*, or to resign his office."

Note I.

It is worthy of remark, that the university of Louvain, which, in answer to the inquiries of Mr Pitt, indignantly disclaimed intolerant and anti-social doctrines, had fourteen years before adopted the theology of Dens, with all its immoral and persecuting principles, as a standard for the guidance of its students. And Dens himself was ALIVE, and one of its members, at the very time that Mr Pitt's questions were proposed, and so indignantly answered ! !

See an able tract of Rev. J. G. Lorimer, entitled "The Theology of Peter Dens, with all its immoral and persecuting principles, proved to be the text book of the present Roman Catholic priesthood of Ireland."

CORRIGENDA.

Page 17, line 19, *for* "discovered," *read* "brought to light."

In same page, line 20, *before* "which," *insert* "some of."

Page 18, line 9, *for* "exhibited," *read* "announced."

ANDREW JACK, PRINTER.

CPSIA information can be obtained
at www.ICGtesting.com
Printed in the USA
BVHW041445160620
581524BV00004B/120

9 780469 411609